Authors' Note

Welcome to our Spriggles family! Spriggles combines "spirit" and "giggles" to motivate young children to lead healthy, active, and enthusiastic lifestyles.

It is important to recognize that while being colorful, playful, and fun, "Spriggles Motivational Books for Children" are, above all else, interactive and educational tools. These are books to be read together by parents and children, grandparents and children, educators and children, and anyone else with a sincere concern for the emotional and physical direction of our kids. As interactive tools, these books enable us to reinforce the positive messages contained on every page. When we read "Reach for the moon, Baboon," it's an ideal time to explain to a child what it means to set a lofty goal and go for it. As well, when we read "It's okay to fail, Whale," it's an ideal time to explain the concept of persistence, as long as the child understands to "Keep on tryin', Lion."

Nota del autor

¡Bienvenidos a la familia Spriggles! Spriggles combina «espíritu» y «risas» para motivar a los niños a llevar vidas saludables, activas, y energéticas.

Es importante reconocer que, aunque coloridos, alegres, y divertidos, «Spriggles: libros motivacionales para niños» son, sobre todo, herramientas interactivas y educativas. Son libros que se debe leer juntos con padres e hijos, abuelos e hijos, maestros y niños, y cualquier otra persona con una preocupación sincera por la dirección emocional de nuestros niños. Como herramientas interactivas, estos libros nos permiten reforzar los mensajes positivos contenidos en cada página. Cuando leemos –Alcanza la luna, Babuino– es un tiempo ideal para explicarles a niños el significado de establecer una meta y lograr para alcanzarla. También, cuando leemos –Está bien fracasar, Ballena–, es un tiempo ideal para explicarles el concepto de la persistencia, mientras que el niño entienda –Sigue intentando, Leona–.

Bobby Baboon has high hopes. Someday he wants to ride a rocket into outer space, but his friends laugh and say it's impossible.

So what do we tell Bobby?

Bobby el babuino tiene grandes esperanzas. Algún día quiere montar un cohete para llegar al espacio exterior, pero sus amigos se ríen y le dicen que es imposible.

¿Pues qué le decimos a Bobby?

"Reach for the moon, Baboon"
-Alcanza la luna, Babuino-

Gerard Saint Bernard wants good grades when he gets to school so he can grow up to be as smart as his mom and dad.

So what do we tell Gerard?

Gerard el perro quiere sacar buenas notas en la escuela para que pueda ser tan listo como Mami y Papi.

¿Pues qué le decimos a Gerard?

"Study hard, Saint Bernard"
-Estudia mucho, Perro-

Izzy Iguana can't seem to make up her mind. She could be a dancer, a teacher, a doctor, and a cheeleader too.

So what do we tell busy Izzy?

Izzy la iguana no puede decidirse. Podría ser bailarina, maestra, doctora, o una porrista también.

¿Pues qué le decimos a Izzy?

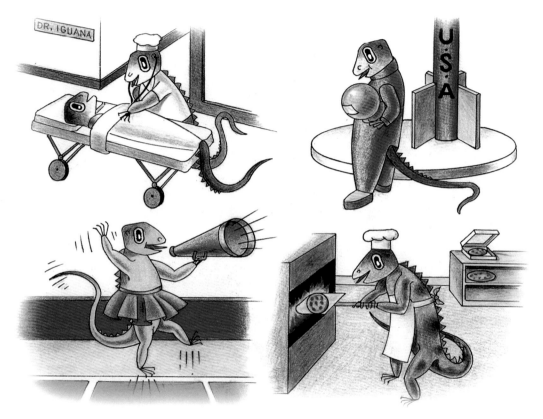

"Be what you wanna, Iguana"

-Sé lo que quieras, Iguana-

Connie Cow knows how to do lots of things. The other cows don't know as much as Connie and ask her for her help.

So what do we tell Connie?

Connie la vaca sabe hacer muchas cosas. Las otras vacas no saben igual que Connie y le piden su ayuda.

¿Pues qué le decimos a Connie?

"Show 'em how, Cow"
–Muéstrales cómo hacerlo, Vaca–

Andy Ant is so hungry that he wants the whole picnic basket, but the basket is so big he's not sure he can carry it.

So what do we tell Andy?

Andy el hormiga tiene tanta hambre que quiere llevarse toda la canasta de picnic, pero es tan grande que no puede hacerlo sólo.

¿Pues qué le decimos a Andy?

"Never say can't, Ant"
-Nunca digas que no, Hormiga-

Lauren Lemur loves to dream about all the things she'd like to do. She hopes that someday her dreams will come true.

So what do we tell snorin' Lauren?

Lauren la lémur le encanta soñar sobre todas las cosas que le gustaría hacer. Ella espera que algún día sus sueños se cumplan.

¿Pues qué le decimos a la relajada Lauren?

"Be a dreamer, Lemur"

-Sé una soñador, Lémur-

Ricky Rhino likes to sleep, but some mornings Ricky sleeps too late and misses the school bus.

So what do we tell Ricky?

Ricky el rinoceronte le gusta dormir, pero en algunas mañanas Ricky duerme demasiado tarde y el autobús le deja.

¿Pues qué le decimos a Ricky?

"Get up and go, Rhino"
–Levántate y ve, Rinoceronte–

Betty Butterfly enjoys the challenge of flying to the tallest flower in the garden.

So what do we tell ready Betty?

Betty la mariposa disfruta del desafío de volar hasta la flor más alta en el jardín.

¿Pues qué le decimos a la lista Betty?

"Aim high, Butterfly"
–Aspira a llegar lejos, Mariposa–

Barry Beaver knows that if he works hard he can reach any goal he sets for himself.

So what do we tell Barry?

Barry el castor sabe que, si trabaja duro, puede lograr cualquier meta que establece para sí mismo.

¿Pues qué le decimos a Barry?

"Be an achiever, Beaver"

-Sé un triunfador, Castor-

Sally Centipede wants to have fun while she is learning.

So what do we tell Sally?

Sally la ciempiés quiere divertirse mientras aprende.

¿Pues qué le decimos a Sally?

"It's fun to read, Centipede"
-Es divertido leer, Ciempiés-

Gary Gazelle is happy because he won third prize at the school science fair, but he's sure he can do better next time.

So what do we tell Gary?

Gary el gacela está feliz porque ganó el premio del tercer lugar en la feria de ciencias en su escuela, pero está seguro que puede mejorar para la próxima vez.

¿Pues qué le decimos a Gary?

"Strive to excel, Gazelle"
–Esfuérzate por alcanzarlo, Gacela–

Jane Great Dane faces a lot of problems that she needs to solve.

So what do we tell Jane?

Jane la gran danés enfrenta los problemas que tiene que resolver.

¿Pues qué le decimos a Jane?

"Use your brain, Great Dane"
-Usa tu inteligencia, Gran Danés-

Paul Polar Bear goes on camping trips with his scout troop. It's important for Paul to plan his trip so he doesn't forget anything.

So what do we tell Paul?

Paul el oso polar sale a acampar con su tropa de niños exploradores. Para Paul, es importante planificar sus viajes para que no se olvide de nada.

¿Pues qué le decimos a Paul?

"Always prepare, Polar Bear"
-Prepara y planifica, Oso Polar-

Pete Porcupine dresses in fancy clothes because it makes him feel special.

So what do we tell neat Pete?

Peter el puercoespín se viste de ropa lujosa porque le hace sentirse especial.

¿Pues qué le decimos al lindo Peter?

"Let yourself shine, Porcupine"
–Brilla y goza, Puercoespín–

Ronald Reindeer is afraid of things he's never done before, but once he tries them he's not afraid anymore.

So what do we tell Ronald?

Ronald el reno teme a las cosas que nunca ha hecho, pero una vez que intenta, no le teme más.

¿Pues qué le decimos a Ronald?

"Conquer your fear, Reindeer"

–Conquista tus miedos, Reno–

Wally Whale gets sad when he tries to jump through the hoop and misses.

So what do we tell Wally?

Wally el ballena se pone triste cuando intenta saltar por el aro y falla.

¿Pues qué le decimos a Wally?

"It's okay to fail, Whale"
–Está bien fracasar, Ballena–

Lulu Lion wants to take her cubs to the top of the mountain, but the mountain is hard to climb and Lulu feels like giving up.

So what do we tell Lulu?

Lulu la leona quiere llevar sus crías a la cima de la montaña, pero la montaña es difícil escalar y Lulu quiere rendirse.

¿Pues qué le decimos a Lulu?

"Keep on tryin', Lion"
–Sigue intentando, Leona–

Homer Hornbill admires the way his uncle builds toy chests and his grandpa tends the garden. Homer would like to do these things too.

So what do we tell Homer?

Homer el pájaro admira cómo su tío construye baúles de juguetes y cómo su abuelo cuida de su jardín. Homer le gustaría hacer éstas actividades también.

¿Pues qué le decimos a Homer?

"Develop a skill, Hornbill"

-Desarrolla un talento, Pájaro-

Liza Lizard enjoys playing with letters and numbers because she finds it magical that they form words and solve problems.

So what do we tell wise Liza?

Liza la lagartija disfruta de jugar con letras y números porque para ella, es mágico cómo forman palabras y resuelven problemas.

¿Pues qué le decimos a Liza?

"Be smart as a wizard, Lizard"
-Sé inteligente, Lagartija-

Pearl Pelican worries about being able to carry enough food to feed her family.

So what do we tell Pearl?

Pearl la pelicano se preocupa sobre su capacidad de cargar suficiente comida para alimentar a su familia.

¿Pues qué le decimos a Pearl?

"Yes you can, Pelican"
-Tú sí puedes, Pelicano-

Sable Squid worked hard to
learn many new things.

So what do we
tell able Sable?

Sable el calamar trabajó duro para
aprender muchas cosas nuevas.

¿Pues qué le decimos
a Sable?

"Be proud of what you did, Squid"

-Sé orgulloso de lo que lograste, Calamar-

Billy Bluebird has lots of good ideas and suggestions, but sometimes he's too shy to say them.

So what do we tell Billy?

Billy el azulejo tiene muchas buenas ideas y sugerencias, pero muchas veces es demasiado tímido para expresarlas.

¿Pues qué le decimos a Billy?

"Make yourself heard, Bluebird"
-Exprésate, Azulejo-

Randy Robin Redbreast is helping his friends build a new nest. Randy enjoys helping others and is always willing to share.

So what do we tell handy Randy?

Randy el petirrojo está ayudando a sus amigos a construir un nido nuevo. Él disfruta de ayudarles a otros y siempre puede compartir.

¿Pues qué le decimos a Randy?

"Be your best, Robin Redbreast"
–Da lo mejor de ti, Petirrojo–

Carla Crocodile is happy most of the time. But sometimes Carla can be sad and wonders how she can feel better.

So what do we tell Carla?

Carla la cocodrilo está feliz la mayoría del tiempo. Pero de vez en cuando se pone triste y quiere saber cómo puede sentirse mejor.

¿Pues qué le decimos a Carla?

"Keep a smile, Crocodile"
–Sigue sonriendo, Cocodrilo–

Knowledge is the
begining of all wisdom

Best Wishes

John Bragg

Oct 22 1931 2.PM

Billericay
England
Essex

51 N 45.
Long 1 W 30.

(Chelmsford.

In Search of Truth

John Everard Bragg

Illustrated

Exposition Press of Florida   *Pompano Beach, Florida*

Dedicated to my children,
their children,
and future generations.

Contents

List of Illustrations

Note to the Reader

The undertaking of the writing of this book was for the benefit of the thinking individual. Its sole purpose is to provoke thought so that one day we may come to a better understanding of the truth. If you are satisfied with traditional religions and your own brand of Christianity; if you can justify the six centuries of terror imposed by the Inquisition which was finally suppressed only a short century and a half ago, and all the religious wars which have been fought down through history; why in Ireland today there is so much hatred between the Catholics and the Protestants; why in the Middle East there is so much enmity between the Jews, Christians and Moslems when we are all worshiping the same God; if you can justify all this then this book may not be for you.

I am taking this opportunity to impress upon the reader the importance of symbolism as you will find symbolism is used extensively throughout the pages of this book. Symbolically speaking, symbolism is a bridge which spans the chasm or spans the void between the physical and the spiritual or the material and the immaterial.

Being human, formed of matter, the only knowledge we can accumulate is through our physical senses: seeing, hearing, feeling, smelling and tasting. Perceiving or sensing individual material things is the kind of knowing which involves the action of our sense organs and our brain; unlike knowing, which involves the physical action of the brain, understanding is a generality. "Seeing is an act of the eye but understanding is not an act of the brain. It is an act of our mind, an immaterial element in our make up that may be related to, but is distinct from, the brain as a material organ." (Page 183, *Aristotle for Everybody,* Mortimer Adler, Macmillan, New York, 1978.)

By sensing with our senses we can perceive an individual material thing such as a bridge: a wooden bridge, a steel bridge, a cement bridge, a large bridge, a small bridge, a bridge over land, or a bridge over water. Our brain allows us to know what a material bridge is. In order to understand the *concept* of a bridge we have to remove the form of the bridge which is the immaterial aspect. That is the thought or idea of a bridge that makes it

ix

possible to understand what the concept of a bridge is from the material which makes it a particular physical bridge. If one were to say, "A bridge between America and England," you would know it was not a material bridge you could walk or drive on but, instead, an immaterial bridge—a concept of a bridge.

We can understand that matter with absolutely no form cannot exist, but that is not true of the opposite. Form can exist without matter, an idea of something is form without matter.

It is only through our sense organs and our brain that we can come to know what is about us in its physical shape. It's our mind which allows us to understand all the aspects of the idea behind all that which is physically created. For an example, we can understand that a bridge can take the shape of anything that will allow something to cross over an otherwise impassable obstacle to reach the other side.

Symbolism is such a bridge, it allows us through the understanding of our mind to cross that void from the physical to the spiritual which by any other means is impossible.

In the following pages, it may appear that I am taking the viewpoint of a male chauvinist but that really is not my intent. Even if I were of the opposite sex, I am sure my reasoning would be the same. By observing the natural, one can come to a better understanding of the supernatural.

To get a better understanding of what I have endeavored to explain, we should answer this question: "Does the human mind introduce an element of immateriality?" Aristotle said it does. "To keep or hold forms separate from matter, the mind itself must be immaterial. If it were material the forms would be kept or held in matter, and then they would no longer be ideas by which we understand things in general." (Page 183, *Aristotle for Everybody*, Mortimer Adler, Macmillan, New York, 1978.)

Introduction

Nothing has confounded the human mind more than the simple questions: "Where did we come from? Where are we going? What is the purpose of our being?"

All peoples of every country have their religions, legends, and their myths. Did each invent their own, independent of each other, or can we find, in our varied legends and myths, a common ancestry bonded together by historical facts, etched in stone standing as witness for some five thousand years only waiting to reveal to us the true identity of the human equivalent of our legendary heroes?

The myths and legends of antiquity are, for the greater part, actual, and factual accounts of the uncomprehensible previous civilization told by a remnant of survivors living through a traumatic experience, handing down their tales to the younger generations not yet significantly regenerated to understand the true meanings.

Although sometimes vague, there seems to be a striking similarity between Gods and heroes of different people.

This book is not intended to be a study of mythology, but myths will be used to unite the races to a common ancestry; as it will be seen most Gods and heroes stem from six original historical figures.

We will find out just who the originals of our heroes and patron saints are, such as King Arthur and his knights of the round table, St. George, and St. Michael; of which the romancing bards took free license of themselves to dramatize. These epic poems are dramatized in a disjointed fashion reducing our history to mere

1

myth and fairy tales. We will even see the originals of our nursery rhyme characters; such as Cinderella, Old Mother Hubbard, and Rumplestiltskin.

The reconstruction and literal translation of the British Edda by L. A. Waddell, LL.D., C.B., C.I.E., has now made it possible to reconstruct the past without the confusion and dogmas of conflicting religions which, I believe, Loki has had a hand in shaping.

I have always been skeptical of the account of creation in Genesis, doubting the validity of the historical facts. A few simple questions one might ask oneself are why did God accept a sanguinary sacrifice from Abel and reject the offering by Cain of the fruits of the field and the labour of his hands; why was Cain marked so no-one would slay him if there was only Adam, Eve and Cain on the earth at that time?

Nevertheless, Cain found a wife and she bore him a son. He named him Enoch and built a city in his honour. I have heard of one horse towns but never a one man city! We also see that the genealogy of Cain and his younger brother Seth are the same up to Noah as reported in Genesis. It appears there are some discrepancies in the first few pages of the Bible; how, then, can we be sure of the remainder?

With access to the many volumes written by scholarly historians and great thinkers, men with inquiring minds who have set their thoughts on paper, I have been inspired by yet another theory as to the beginnings of man. This theory is supported by reason and braced by historical facts. Let these facts with logical reasoning lead where they will.

Here is something to bear in mind, Ecclesiastes, 1:9–11: "The thing that hath been, it *is that* which shall be; and that which is done *is* that which shall be done: and *there is* no new *thing* under the sun. Is there *any* thing whereof it may be said, See, this *is* new? it hath been already of old time, which was before us. *There is* no remembrance of former *things;* neither shall there be *any* remembrance of *things* that are to come with *those* that shall come after."

It is the object of this book to provoke thought in the direction of truth and the mystery of life and for people to realize, as individuals and nations, who they must stand behind and give their support to. It is also to remind those given the responsibility of maintaining peace and guiding the nations not to neglect their mundane duties by giving themselves over too completely to their spiritual duties.

We must also realize that the scriptures quoted above are to be taken literally; every experience we may have had, everything invented or discovered, or everything that is or will be, has been before. The cycles of history are the basics from which this theory springs. To put this theory in its right perspective so it can be comprehended more easily one should find a high place on a mountain where you can command a good overview of the forest as a whole. If you go down amongst the trees you may get confused, even lost. The trees create obstacles, shortening your vision, making it virtually impossible for you to get a clear, overall picture of the forest.

CHAPTER 1

The Creation

The geography of the planet Earth was considerably different in antediluvian times than it is today. It was populated by a primitive aboriginal people, the ancestors of the Semitic races. They inhabited an area of the Earth where life could be maintained with a minimum of effort. They were a very small black-headed race, probably standing about four feet tall. They lived in burrows under the ground (living in darkness under the ground in hell). The literal translation of the word Hell or Hades is a cellar or hole in the ground away from light—a place where evil thrives. *Encyclopedia Americana:* the abode of evil spirits where the devil rules supreme.

The serpent worshiping matriarch, El of Eden; also known as Mary, Ymi, Gulli, Heidi and Ida; and Wodan, her consort, an aboriginal; also known by the name Bodo; and their son Abel; also known by the names of Loki, Baldr, Lucifer and Seth; were the ruling cast, forming the Eden Triad.

For fear of losing control over their Semitic subjects, education was denied them. They were kept in fear, ignorance, and suppression; sacrifices were introduced, both animal and human, to animal gods; namely the lion, wolf and serpent. Anyone found not worshiping their holy wolves was put to death. The same penalty applied to anyone acquiring any knowledge of her eerie rune secrets, or voicing their opinions.

Their cauldron, or well of knowledge, was kept from the people to confound them and cause them to believe in superstitions and

5

magic. Thus the origin of the witches cauldron handed down in our fairy tales.

It is evident by the presence of uncivilized and underdeveloped tribes of aborigines in this age, without tapping the source of all knowledge, that they have remained in their primitive state steeped in superstition honouring their animal gods for thousands of years. Living witnesses of the first created man, as we shall see later.

There are two lines of thought on the human origin, did man ascend the ladder of evolution from one cell to the complex intelligent being of today or was he created?

I see no continuity of life from the simple to the complex; I see no cornerstone on which to build, no concrete foundations for the theory of evolution. So I will concentrate on the latter. Creation still poses an unanswerable question. If God created man, who created God? That question is beyond our powers of comprehension. Until such time when all things are understood we will have to be satisfied with the question of who created us. Whoever created us is infinitely superior and automatically demands our respect and worship; therefore, he is our God and we will have to answer to none other.

It is not for us to create our God in our image, but to use what intelligence we are given to constructively put together an image with all the fragmented bits of information we can gather from all the writings and legends from ancient times so we can know our creator.

Scientists are unraveling the mysteries of the universe, time, space, the molecular structure of matter, even the amino acid chain of life itself. Knowledge is exploding at an ever accelerating rate.

Is it not reasonable, in the light of what we have learned, to re-examine the past and apply our knowledge of today to the mysteries that confounded our forefathers.

If our creator is the all powerful, omnipresent God as some suppose, he would not have had to, as stated in Genesis 11:5, "came down to see the city and the tower, which the children of men builded." He would have known without making a special trip.

What do you suppose Ezekiel is describing when he describes the cherubim? The cherubim, according to *Webster's New Collegiate Dictionary,* is a holy place often represented with wings. This holy place apparently has wheels flies in the air and fire flashes from it. R.S.V. Ezekiel 10:16–17 "And when the cherubim went, the wheels went beside them; and when the cherubim lifted up their wings to mount up from the earth, the wheels did not turn from beside them. When they stood still, these stood still, and when they mounted up, these mounted up with them; for the spirit of the living creatures was in them. And also Elijah, 2 Kings 2:11, was taken into heaven in a chariot of fire. As Elisha reports he was taken up in a whirlwind, possibly the take off of the chariot caused a strong wind.

Is it not reasonable then for us to suppose that when God came down to see the tower of Babel he may have come in a cherubim, a chariot of fire, or maybe a space craft of some kind.

Is it not reasonable for earth bound people to suppose that any direction away from this earth is up, it is only recently that we refer to leaving the earth as going out into space.

There are repeated accounts in the Bible where beings come down to and go up from this earth. From where did they come and to where do they go?

It is not unreasonable to assume then that they have a dwelling on another planet in another universe. It is also not unreasonable to think that they closely resemble us; with the exception that they are thousands of years technologically advanced in science; so far so that it is beyond our comprehension to imagine the advances they have made.

Along this line of reasoning it is also possible to assume that the Star of Bethlehem could have been an UFO sent to guide the three wise men. There have been many accounts of sightings of UFO's seen as bright lights even in recent times. It is certainly worthy of consideration.

In the depths of the dark ages, when the Catholic Church was at its apex, all knowledge was suppressed; great libraries were destroyed; any new thought was hearsay and punishable by torture, imprisonment, or death. It was very fortunate, or was it by design, that a grand master of the keepers of the secrets of the Holy Grail, or sometimes called the Mountain Stone, should appear at that time to save civilization from sinking even further into the abyss of ignorance and superstition.

Some authorities trace the beginnings of the Renaissance to the early fourteenth century Italian poet Alighieri Durante, also known as Dante; others attribute the first major impulse to the Italian poet Petrarch (Francesco Petracco), but it was in the early 1400's that the Renaissance started to gain momentum. It would not be inaccurate to suggest that René d'Anjou was an impetus behind the phenomenon of the Renaissance. The freedom of speech and freedom of religion are among our most treasured possessions. It is a shame, but a fact of this world, that the subtler powers that be that are warring amongst us have granted us another freedom, a freedom to abuse our freedoms.

Our Grand Master, Jesus Christ, the keeper of the secrets of the Holy Grail, when asked why he spoke in parables answered, "It is only given to those who have eyes to see and ears to hear that can understand." So then he proceeded to explain that most people without thinking assume that Jesus withheld the meanings of the parables to the crowds and explained the meaning only to his disciples. This is lacking in logic. If Jesus was only speaking to the elite, those with eyes to see and ears to hear, he would not have had to explain them to his disciples, as they were the elite and they would have understood. And why would Jesus have discriminated against a few hundred that were listening to him then and not tell them the meaning, and then have the parables recorded in the Bible, complete with their meanings, for countless of millions to read. Therefore the parable was no longer a secret, so we see the parable is a parable within a parable. The true meaning is the fact that all of Jesus's teachings have hidden meanings, so only the elect who have eyes to see and ears to hear will understand. This made it more difficult for those who assumed the responsibility of editing and compiling the scriptures to alter or pervert them, if they did not understand the true meanings. Matthew 13:35—"I will open my mouth in parables; I will utter things which have been kept secret from the foundation of the world."

According to the quote above Jesus is going to reveal to us the truth of the beginnings of this world, hitherto unknown to us. So we should not be shocked if what we learn is new to us and somewhat contrary to what has been accepted.

It is impossible for any of us to know exactly what happened in the beginning, all we have is a few facts to speculate with. Namely, the world is millions of years old, there were dinosaurs roaming on the earth at one time, there was vegetation in the arctic regions, that this world has suffered some great upheavals, and the fact that we, mankind, are on this earth today.

In order to arrive at a starting place I will begin with a story, purely from my imagination, while we progress through the ages until we come to the first signs of recorded history.

Many thousands of years ago, in the far reaches of space, there was a planet. On this planet there was life very much the same as we know it, only much further advanced in knowledge, science, and the art of living. There was no sickness, no wars, no sorrow, no pain; in fact it was void of all sin, as it is only sin which is the cause of all sorrow. They had reached the plane of perfection. They were not always perfect; when they were created their God spent a lot of time and love teaching them the secrets of obtaining eternal life. Through the application of the moral code, otherwise known as the ten commandments, and the complete adherence to them, they soon noticed that the causes of war were no longer present, and war became a thing of the past. All twelve kings united and formed one central government which worked together for the well-being of every nation.

Working together in peace and harmony, pooling their knowledge and resources, there was no end to their imagination of what they proposed to do. Their life became a continuous joy of creativeness and accomplishment, ever learning, ever expanding their horizons. They had perfected space travel and it was now possible to travel at the speed of light, making time virtually stand still.

They had discovered the very germ of life, the amino acid chain, and understood the intricate workings of genetics. This led them to the capability of creating life.

In previous voyages into space they had discovered a planet which was very much like their own. It would support life as they knew it, but it was void.

The necessary elements and climatic conditions were there. Upon further investigation it was decided it would make a perfect laboratory. It would be far enough away and remote enough that if anything went contrary to their plans and the result of their creation became a Frankenstein it would be earth bound and unable to affect their way of life in their utopia, their planet which they had named Heaven.

Their first experiment was to create the plant life. It was very complicated and took considerably more than one of our twenty four hour days, probably more like one thousand years. Then the idea of the dinosaurs, the giant reptiles, was conceived; they were laboriously developed using the life giving energy of the sun to motivate them, very much on the same order as the plants. They were quite pleased with their creation for awhile, but they soon got bored with the big ugly creatures.

Through experiments they decided they could create superior creatures, the warm blooded mammals; so in order to make a habitat for their new warm blooded mammals it was decided that by using a gigantic nuclear blast the earth could be tilted on its axis causing a complete change in climatic conditions, resulting in flooding and devastation, destroying all the reptiles of their first creation and preparing a new world for their new creation.

The vegetation was recreated and some of the smaller, more efficient reptiles were created. The new warm blooded animals were made. All this wasn't made in a day, it appears to have taken about one thousand years to complete each step. As we see one of the secrets of the Holy Grail has been unveiled to us in II Peter 3:8 "But, beloved, be not ignorant of this one thing, that one day *is* with the Lord as a thousand years, and a thousand years as one day."

Einstein's theory of relativity has made it possible for us to understand that with inter-galactic travel at the speed of light time can be made to stand still. The secrets of the Holy Grail are metered out to us, little by little, in the hope that as we learn the secrets of the universe we will be mature and civilized enough to handle these truths for our growth and advancement and not our destruction, as was the case of the previous civilization. Alas, we still seem to be in our swaddling clothes.

They saw what they had done and they said it was very good. Now, however, they had one more challenge, the biggest step of all; could they re-create themselves, could they make man in their own image? They had contemplated on proceeding along the same lines as they had done with the warm blooded animals; but to implant their own character, their own intellect, their own mind with the creativeness and imagination which they possessed, posed a problem. As it is understood, it is impossible to make anything equal to or superior to the one who is making it.

Nevertheless, it was decided by the Commander-in-Chief or the King of United Heaven that this final and most important project of their creation should be attempted.

A summit meeting of all twelve kingdoms of United Heaven was called, and it was decided that a united effort would be made. Each kingdom would contribute a work force in the field where they were the most qualified. This united effort was headed by one named Adam, the son of the king.

The system of government in Heaven was a kingdom, it was governed from the top by the King and he was assisted by his staff of advisors. This central government had delegates installed in each of the twelve kingdoms to keep in touch with the pulse of the nations so if any problems should arise the central government could rule on it with the best interests of all in mind.

Freedom was of prime importance, each person was free to contribute whatever he saw fit for society, each person received reward according to their effort. There was no graft, no corruption or greed. Honesty and integrity had become part of their nature. It had become virtually impossible for them to transgress the law because by this time, in their advanced state, the very thoughts of a man could be perceived—not reading the mind thought by thought, or word for word, but to perceive whether a man's thoughts were honourable, whether they were devious, whether his plans were for the good of all or whether they were selfish thoughts intent on satisfying his own greed, lusts, and vanity. When a man's thoughts were perceived to be dishonest, no one would deal with him. He would automatically be ostracized until he cast his sinful thoughts out of his mind. Now, if you don't harbour evil thoughts in your mind it is impossible to do evil as it is your thoughts that govern your actions.

Matthew 9:3 "And behold, certain of the scribes said within themselves, This *man* blasphemeth." Jesus, however, knowing their thoughts, said, "Why do you think evil in your hearts?" This is an example that the perception of a man's thoughts was quite normal for Jesus.

The project on Earth had proceeded as scheduled, everything had gone well, all according to plan. The Commander-in-Chief of Heaven (later known as God the Father by the created) announced that the mission was accomplished. They had successfully created a living being in their image who was genetically compatible to themselves, he was on a plane above the animals, he was a free moral agent, and he had the ability to think for himself; but he was on a considerably lesser plane than his creators. He was limited in his imagination and his creative abilities, he was small in stature, about four feet tall, and was dark with black hair.

This announcement called for a celebration, creation had been completed. Job 38:7 ". . . and all the sons of God shouted for joy." The work was completed and the work force was returning home to Heaven. Everyone was celebrating and shouting for joy at their achievement.

Adam, on completion of their creation, left planet Earth and headed home to Heaven with eleven of the representatives of the kingdom. The twelfth, El, and about one third of the workers remained.

El had grown fond of the new creation which she had helped with, she had a desire for it. In her mind, harmless enough at first, she entertained thoughts of grandeur, imagining herself as Commander-in-Chief answerable to no-one, appointing her chosen followers to high places in her government. What a wonderful place she could make of this Earth if she could rule it the way she planned. She enlisted followers, promising favoured positions of authority for their allegiance, thus sowing the seeds of greed, vanity, and covetousness. The breaking of the law constitutes sin. The laws had been broken, sin had been introduced to this world by El. That could have been the original true source of the phrase: "woman was the downfall of man."

As you no doubt know; but it is worth a little thought; a little pure water in a barrel of polluted water will not purify it, but a little polluted water in a barrel of fresh water will pollute all of it.

It is that way with sin. For a good example, if someone tells a minor untruth, another lie must be told in order to cover up until eventually you are telling nothing but lies. The only way out is to come clean, confess the truth, and start afresh.

CHAPTER 2

The Deterioration
of the Creation

We are now slipping from the realms of speculation and imagination into the world of reason, documented by historical records dating back approximately to 3378 B.C.

My theories are based to a large extent on the works of the very accomplished Lawrence Austin Waddell. I don't believe Lawrence Waddell realized all the ramifications involved when he traced the King lines with dates, dynasties, their monuments and their accomplishments from the end of known history, 1736 B.C. back to 3378 B.C. Documented in great detail in his book titled *The Makers of Civilization,* and also with the publication of the *British Edda,* still further secrets have been unveiled of the ancient past, even as far back as the beginning.

When the matriarch, El, took over the power from the Commander-in-Chief of Heaven, and implanted herself as supreme ruler in complete authority of the newly created kingdom, all went well for awhile. There was something lacking, though. These newly created human beings lacked imagination, creativeness, to state it plainly these created human beings were just barely above the animal plane. They could think and reason a little, but just enough to satisfy their immediate needs. They had no vision, after all they only had the spirit *created* by their creators and not the spirit *of* their creators. To remedy this and further upgrade their

14

creation, inter-breeding was practised. The result of this was a vigorous hybrid being with some of the intellect and imagination of the creators and the carnal pull of the flesh, the desire to preserve and satisfy their physical needs and desires. Gen. 6:4 ". . . when the sons of God came in unto the daughters of men, and they bare *children* to them, the same *became* mighty men which *were* of old, men of renown." The mighty men referred to here doesn't mean they were evil or righteous, it means that they had taken on another dimension by possessing some of the spirit of God, making them not only God's creation but also sons and heirs. As we see later in this passage, Gen. 6:4 in the Bible does not refer only to the matriarch, El, and her followers inter-breeding with man, but we see later on in the Edda that Adam allowed this same practice to upgrade man.

Fig. 1—Wodan or Bodo, consort of Ymi or Heidi in Egyptian myth as *Butan* or *Patah* ("Ptah") consort of Hether (Heidi), as primeval progenitor of aborigines, represented as naked bandy-legged dwarf. (After *British Edda,* L.A. Waddell.)

Fig. 2—Nursing Serpent Mother-Matriarch in Egyptian myth as *Rann-t = Rann,* title of Heidi or Ymi in Edda. Note she is given the head of her Serpent totem, the hooded serpent or cobra. (After *British Edda,* L.A. Waddell.)

Note in Fig. 2 that we see the matriarch, El; herself impregnated by an aboriginal man. From Egyptian myth we see Butan or Ptah depicted as a bandy-legged dwarf. Butan is the equivalent of Wodan or Bodo, El's consort; with their son Loki or Baldr (Abel) thus forming the Eden Triad.

The utopian kingdom which El had envisioned was not materializing, having set the foundations of the kingdom on sand (on sin) and not on rock (truth and righteousness) it was already starting to crumble. As I mentioned, one lie requires another as a little polluted water will pollute the whole barrel, so it was with their kingdom.

Education of the Edenities ceased, El could see this new breed of man had no limits, it would only be a matter of time when they would be her equal. Knowing she had taken Earth from the King of Heaven herself, she was afraid man would do likewise to her. Seeing this as an inevitability, she saw man as a Frankenstein, threatening her very existence. The only way she could control man was to suppress him and keep him in ignorance, steeped in superstition and in awe of her knowledge, thinking it to be magic. In order to accomplish this more sins were introduced; deception, jealousy, selfishness, greed, hatred; each previous sin introduced the next. In a short time they were well acquainted with all nine heads of the Hydra.

Gods were invented, harsh and unyielding, requiring human sacrifices to appease them. Superstitions were invented, animals were deemed sacred, the lion, wolf and serpent and also the raven. In the stead of a blossoming kingdom it was on its way to dying; steeped in ignorance, superstition, fear, squalor and near starvation. And, like today, they didn't really know why.

This situation parallels the Dark Ages when one power rose to supremacy in Western Eruope and for fear of losing their power suppressed their subjects, plunging them into the depths of ignorance and superstition.

The new creation was fast becoming a disaster. A decision was reached in Heaven. Adam was to return to Earth with the original work force from eleven of the kingdoms in Heaven to restore order, uplift, develop, and civilize the new creation; and take over the rulership from the matriarch El. To accomplish this Adam returned to Earth incarnate as a mortal being.

It is not my intent to fictionalize our beginnings or discredit our religions or detract from the sincerity of our beliefs. It is my intent, however, to attempt to explain some of the mysteries and misconceptions of the past that many of the religions of this world are based on by the use of documented historical facts, myths and legends.

If, by applying twentieth century reasoning to the past, we can bring into focus that which would otherwise be just sanctimonious ritual, little understood, and rekindle the interest of the agnostic or otherwise twentieth century free thinkers who have given up the teachings of the Bible as a collection of outdated writings which might have served a purpose at one time, but do not apply to us in this modern age.

For an example, if we apply our twentieth century thinking to some of the old scriptures we can look at Gen. 11:6 in the light of what we know now, "And the Lord said, Behold the people *is* one, and they have all one language; and this they begin to do: and now nothing will be restrained from them, which they have imagined to do."

This being, our God, did in fact come down from the Heavens to see what man (his creation who he created in his likeness in appearance, form and mind) was doing and said, "Nothing they put their minds to will be impossible for them to accomplish."

Man will have the same creative powers as his creator, and if you bear in mind Gen. 6:4 ". . . when the sons of God came in unto the daughters of men, and they bare *children* to them, . . .", not only are we created in his likeness, but we are also his sons and daughters.

Man has already set his mind to exploring space, and is intrigued with the possibility of eventually creating life. If man can learn the causes of war, and avoid the trap of self-destruction, given enough time living in peace and devoting all his energies to the accumulation of knowledge, eventually all things being possible, we will perfect space travel and will be scientifically advanced enough to create life.

The day will come when we will locate a planet suitable to sustain life. *We* will be shouting for joy at the completion of the creation of a new world, then we will be Gods ourselves over our creation, and on it goes.

CHAPTER 3

Lemuria and Atlantis

The cradle of creation was the Garden of Eden. Such a place had to be prepared for man to insure his survival. The Garden of Eden was situated in the Pacific Ocean on a continent which no longer exists. This continent is known today as the lost continent of Lemuria, or sometimes referred to as Mu, meaning Motherland. There also was the island continent of Atlantis which also has since sunk beneath the waters of the Atlantic, lost forever.

I won't dwell on the proof of the existence of either of these continents as it has been well established that they did in fact exist prior to the recorded history dating back to the time of the great flood, some three thousand years B.C.

There have been many titles on the subject. For further study for those who wish documented proof I can recommend two works, which I believe to be most enlightening. Firstly, *The Lost Continent of Mu*, by Churchward, and *Atlantis: Antediluvian World* by Ignatious Donnelly, 1981, Harper & Row, paperback edition. I do not share his views on all points but I do believe the proof of Atlantis' existence has been well documented.

In the days when Lemuria and Atlantis flourished land masses bridged what are now the oceans, allowing man to spread both east and west with considerable ease as they had no vast oceans to navigate. They could travel by land with only short distances to be navigated by boat or raft. I am not suggesting that at this early time all the world was populated, but it is feasible to assume that some tribes had ventured to other lands, Atlantis in particular.

Lemuria was truly a Garden of Eden. It was, as I mentioned, the cradle of creation, everything that man required was there. Food was abundant, minerals were in profusion in the ground, forests of magnificent trees were readily available for lumber, quarries of beautiful stone were plentiful for the construction of buildings. It was still all going to waste. Man; under the rulership of the matriarch, El of Eden, the Serpent Priestess, her consort Wodan, their son Abel, and the three Fate Weirds of Eden; was fast degenerating. They were suppressed and kept in ignorance and fear with no moral code, no light to guide them, they had become savages.

At this point in time the Aryan Sumerian, or more accurately named Goths, appeared in Atlantis. They referred to themselves as Goths. Goth means Goat, their motif is the Goat as opposed to the Lion, Wolf, and Serpent totems of the Edenites.

This is the beginning of the war, the battle between good and evil. This war has been waged since the beginning of time, since King Adam-Thor's return with his Aryans to civilize and uplift man and win the creation back from the Matriarch El and her Edenites. El is furious, she jealously resents Adam-Thor. She is too proud to admit her mistake and she still holds fast to her belief that man will take over if given the chance; he is a monster controlled only by suppression. El has been banned from returning to Heaven because of her transgressions and she would be an outcast on Earth if her fears were realized and man was regenerated and taught by Adam-Thor.

Adam-Thor, on the other hand, believes that man; when civilized, educated in the moral code, and allowed to accumulate knowledge; will eventually realize the purpose of his being, will become their equal and attain perfection.

This is the basis for the battle between good and evil down through the ages. God on the one hand wants to increase man's knowledge to give him every opportunity to qualify into the kingdom as his son and heir. Satan, on the other hand, maintains that man is a Frankenstein and if allowed to increase in knowledge will become uncontrollable and eventually become their oppressors.

Satan is battling to preserve their kingdom on Earth and doing everything in his power to retard man's advancement; with every new achievement comes an undesirable side effect—Pandora's Box Syndrome. Working through human's; appealing to their baser nature of selfishness, envy, and hate; he thwarts the best laid plans of God and man.

Most of the artifacts, such as rock carvings and sun temples, were found in Asia Minor and Mesopotamia, that being the center of civilization at the beginning of our recorded history. Nevertheless, there seem to be recordings of events which happened before that time. Names in those times, as in these times, are carried from the old world to the new world, as you find many cities in the America's named after cities in Britain and Europe. If, for example, England were to sink beneath the North Sea and some thousands of years later some documentation of a city by the name of London was found, the archaeologist would, no doubt, associate it with their diggings of an ancient city they had uncovered in Canada by that name. The same could very easily apply to the old world, the survivors of the lost continents would no doubt bring their old familiar names with them to the new land.

The history of ancient times has been laboriously traced back to 3378 B.C. by comparing and cross checking the two old Sumerian king lists; the Isin chronicles, preserving the four hundred thirty year gap in the Kish Chronicle, and also by discovering that the Kassi dynasty of Babylonia was an Aryan dynasty; by cross checking these king lists by name, deeds, accomplishments, monuments, and seals dates with the official Indian Aryan King list. Presenting undeniable proof of a continuous chronology with dates and names of the Sumerian Aryan or Nordic Kings, the "Goths"; thereby disclosing the dates from Odin Thor, the original King Ar-Thur or St. George or King Adam, from about 3378 B.C. with regnal years down to the classic period and the date of Menes as 2704 B.C. (Ref. *Makers of Civilization* by L.A. Waddell, Chapter XXVI.)

Now we have the human equivalent, the historically documented equivalent, of King Arthur and St. George, the patron saint of Cappadocia and merry England, as being Adam of the old testament and St. Michael or Sir Gawain as King Adam's son Cain.

The truth has a habit of surfacing from time to time, whether by accident or by design nevertheless it does, and keeps us from being blown too far off course through the voyage of life and time. We sometimes have to make a navigational change as much as one hundred eighty degrees, which we find very difficult both to do and to admit to ourselves that we have been sailing along in the wrong direction for so long at a time.

The heroic poems of our ancient heroes, or epics, with their champion making deeds of valor shed a new light of truth. A record of ancient history which has been sleeping for centuries in the remote vastness of Iceland, preserved and protected, hidden away from the rampaging early Christian fanatical missionaries whose sole purpose was to destroy the accumulation of knowledge contained in the ancient Briton Manuscripts, and stigmatizing them as pagan, has been recovered.

These ancient manuscripts have now been reconstruced by L.A. Waddell in their original form as the British Edda. It has been restored from the jumbled and disjointed medieval manuscript to it's current form in the Dark Ages sometime around the ninth century A.D. It was modernized by Geoffrey of Monmouth and Robert Wace the Anglo-Norman in the twelfth century. It was later popularized by Chaucer, Malory, Wadsworth, Tennyson and other Bards romancing the deeds of King Arthur, St. George of England with his Red Cross, and Sir Gawain and the Holy Grail; adapting them to the christian legend and consequently turning into myth the *allegorical* history of thousands of years before the christian period.

It has been proven by L.A. Waddell in his work *The Makers of Civilization* that a direct lineage of kings does exist, unbroken, back to the beginning of recorded history. The first king was King Zagg, Gaur, Adar, or, as we are most familiar with, Adam.

Adam was deified as the Sun God by King Khammu Rabi in 2000 B.C. (Fig. 3, page 23.) He is depicted on the top of diorite stele as giving King Khammu Rabi the law code from which our ten commandments were written by Moses, with the exception of the fourth which proclaims the Sabbath as holy.

For the complete list of Sumerian, or early Aryan kings, in Sumerian names and the equivalency in Indian see pages 482–5, *Makers of Civilization*, 1929, by L.A. Waddell.

KING KHAMMU RABI RECEIVING THE LAW FROM
THE SUN-GOD, *c.* 2000 B.C.

Fig. 3—Top of diorite stele of this king's Law Code, now in the Louvre.
This monument, 8 ft. high, inscribed with 44 cols. of Laws, aggregating
2644 lines, originally set up in the temple of Marduk at Babylon, was
found at Susa, whither it had been carried as an Elam raid-trophy. The
sculptures in bas-relief on its top, besides portraying the king with
straight non-Semitic nose, represent the seated Sun-god (the deified
1st Sumer king) of fine Aryan type, bearded, long-locked and wearing
a Phrygian hat, adorned with four horns (set in sockets). A Lotus flower,
the symbol of the Sun-god and the name of the king (Khammu Rabi),
is seen above the god's head near the margin of the tone, and between
its two chipped portions. (After *Makers of Civilization*, L.A. Waddell.)

Cain, the son of King Adam, was the second king; also known as Gan at Enoch City or Nimrod, later deified as St. Michael, the Arch Angel.

There is a period in the very early history which has been confusing and has been rejected as inaccurate recording by the Isin priests. There appeared in the Isin priests chronicles earlier dynasties with fabulous ages which were prefixed to the first Sumerian dynasty of the Kish chronicle. They were supposed, by an Assyriologist scholar to be records of the Antediluvian dynasty; but I quote from page 127 of *The Makers of Civilization*, "These dynasties prefixed to the Kish Chronicle by the credulous myth-mongering priests of Isin are betrayed by their own records to be merely duplications of the First and Second Dynasties of the Kish Chronicle which have been arbitrarily misplaced in front of the latter."

I believe that some of this confusion could be accredited to the two first kings deified as God and Arch Angel, having ruled in both the Antidiluvian and post-diluvian ages. It has been proven that Cain and Nimrod are one and the same. So, King Cain lived and ruled before the great flood and also after the flood. This could very easily account for King Cain having ruled in both the first and second dynasties. The first being on Atlantis and after the flood or the destruction of Atlantis he set up his kingdom in Asia Minor, at Enoch on the Euphrates River.

CHAPTER 4

The Prologue to the Edda

The minstrel Sibyl (fortune teller and prophet) sings the epics on deeds of valor of our ancient heroes and their constant struggle between good and evil down through the ages.

It was a custom at holidays and festivals to honour the heroes of bygone days in this manner. The importance of passing down the history, keeping it alive and in the minds of all, both great and common folk, was tremendous and with the ending of each lay the words:

> *Know ye yet the Edda?*
> *Know ye yet it all?*

There has been some confusion concerning the name *Edda* as the title of this collection of ancient poetry revealing our history. It has been associated with the Icelandic word Mother or Grandmother, dubbing the Edda's as Icelandic mythology. It has been revealed, not withstanding the fact that the Edda's were preserved in Iceland during the rampages of early Christendom, the name Edda spelled with one d—Eda—appears in the earliest of the Sibyl lays. Eda is probably derived from the word Veda, the title of the collection of hymns and writings in sanskrit of the Eastern Aryans which deal with the same deified God Indra, a title of King Adam Thor of the Edda's.

Veda in Sanskrit; from Vid: meaning to see, perceive, or know; would seem to mean (in the Gothic term Eda) to have knowledge of the history of our beginning.

25

There may be some discrepancies in the order and sequence of some of the scenes of the Edda and some of the subtle symbolic meanings are not too clear, but generally speaking there is a story thread woven through the lays with a more profound, prophetic meaning than first appears. Most of the lays, if taken at literal value, would not be history making material. With a little imagination one can get quite a revealing story of the beginning of man's existence on Earth and his many trials and tribulations and his battles between good and evil. Sometimes winning and sometimes losing; portrayed in the Edda as when Satan is wounded or bound good prevails, or when Adam or Cain is wounded or bound evil prevails.

The minstrel Sibyl in the second verse claims to have a God given gift of second sight, not only can she see the past but over every world (age or time, past or future).

Part One

SCENE I
THE EDEN TRIAD

Scene I is a description of the Matriarch of Eden and Edenites at their lowest, degenerate ebb in a world of evil; despondent, wretched and with no hope, all their efforts amount to naught in their sinful debased state. Scene I goes on to tell the story of how they became in that condition.

To keep control over her subjects El kept them in ignorance and superstition. She declared lions, wolves and serpents sacred, no doubt because of the qualities they possessed. She admired the lion for it's strength and power, the wolf for it's vicious and cunning nature and the serpent for it's venomous nature and also because it sheds it's skin annually, the reason that native tribes of South America worship the snake to this day, representing to them immortality.

She has close around her her council, the three Weirds. They adore and respect her for her ability to perform witchery, she calls them her bad, brothel brides.

The tyranny by which she ruled is demonstrated here . . . "The penalty for anyone confuting her, or killing one of her holy wolves, or even learning any of her mystic spells, was death by torture."

El takes an aboriginal named Wodan, or Bodo, and produces a son, Wolf Loki (Baldr or Abel), by him. He is called the slippery one, that Adder-Thaughted scarer with his all fearful lust.

The Edenites at that time were known to be of the Chaldeans and Semitic race; they were all black headed, dark complexioned people. Strife and war reigned among them as shown in this lay . . .

Atrocities of the Serpent Priestess

Hurt reigned in her home
And much houridom (whoredom).
A club-age, an axe-age
With butchery cleaving.
A wind-age, a wolf-age,
Ere the old world riot was stopt:
Men tore other men untiring.

Fig. 4—Internecine strife in Eden. From Sumer seal *c.* 3000 B.C., Note Sumerian sign in front of the archer (Egil or Baldr) reads *Edin* or *Etin* (*i.e.,* "Eden"), and the sign in front of the man with uplifted club reads, "The Wolf's Mate." (After *British Edda,* L.A. Waddell.)

Wodan, El, and Loki are not only in Cappadocian and Mesopotamian legends. They also appear in Hindu, British, Egyptian
and Greek mythology, forming a common origin for our myth.

Fig. 5—The She-wolf Mother Ymi or Kali (Ymi, Kiol, Gulli or El of Edda)
as Ogress in Indian tradition. From nineteenth-century Indian picture.
(In Wilkins' *Hindu Mythology.*) The nether Ogress sucked mankind in
misfortunes: The She-wolf Frigg slit the men (divided men). (After *British Edda,* L.A. Waddell.)

SCENE II
KING ADAM RETURNS

King Adam; Her-Thor or Ar-Thur the Goth; with his Aryan's
returned to regenerate and civilize the world, 3380 B.C.

Plato said he was told by Solon, who in turn was told by an
ancient Egyptian priest, that the island continent of Atlantis once
stood to the west out through the Gates of Hercules. He went on
to describe it, then he concluded that the island sank into the sea
leaving mud and debris in its wake making the sea unnavigable
beyond the Gates of Hercules. It was to this land of Atlantis where
King Adam Thor came with his Aryans, or Goths, and established
his reign of reason.

791

Fig. 6—King Thor, Sig, Odo, or Adam. From Hittite stele. Note he is bearded, in Gothic dress with shaven upper lip, horned hat, long boots with turned-up toes, carrying in his right hand his Hammer and in left Fire-torch. (After *British Edda*, L.A. Waddell.)

Fig. 7—King Thor or Odo as Sumerian deified King Udu or Odo, the Sun-god. From King Khammu Rabi's Law-code stele, *c.* 2000 B.C. Note his fine Aryan type, shaven upper lip, Gothic horned hat. (After *British Edda*, L.A. Waddell.)

The Aryans were of the Caucasian race. Adam Thor was described as being tall, red bearded, golden haired and blue eyed. The great white race.

It was this first Sumerian or early Aryan king who established Sun-worship as part of his system of civilization (page 23, *Makers of Civilization*). Worshipping the sun as sustainer of life symbolized the sun as representing the one all powerful God. Later King Dar or Adam-Thor was deified as the son of the Sun-god and later the second king, the son of the first, was deified as the Arch Angel of the Sun-god under the title of Mukuon Muk Kla, the invincible warrior who has been proven as the historical human Sumerian original of our St. Michael the Archangel (p 24, *Makers of Civilization*) proving the Eddas to be historical and not mythological as supposed.

When I refer to Sun-worship as the true religion of Adam Thor and of this world some may have difficulty in understanding what sun worship really is. It is symbolized by the cross. The cross represents the sacred four. The sacred four are the four basic elements contained in the sun—carbon, oxygen, nitrogen and hydrogen, which all matter is made from.

The sun is the light of this world and also the sustenance of life. Symbolically the sun is light enabling us to see where we are going versus darkness where we cannot and lose direction, resulting in stagnation in ignorance and superstition. Light is enlightenment or knowledge, knowledge is truth; so basically Sun-worship is the search for truth. "There is no religion higher than truth."

The Bible gives more than a little hint that the sun and it's light is representative of God the Creator and is the sustenance of life and the light of truth. (Isaiah 60:20) "The sun shall be no more thy light by day; . . . but the Lord shall be unto thee an everlasting light, . . ." and Matthew 17:02—"And was transfigured before them: and his face did shine as the sun, and his raiment was white as the light." There are numerous other references in the Bible where light and truth are synonymous with God.

The moon cults referred to in the Edda are in semi-darkness. They have but a little light, just a mere pale reflection of the light of the sun.

This one God concept was opposed to the Eden Triad's numerous Gods whom they invented and who were harsh and unyielding. They were continuously trying to appease them by sanguinary animal and human sacrifices.

The True Cross, the Sun-Cross, or the Red Cross of St. George of Cappadocia and England (p 16, *Makers of Civilization*), which was a cross made from the sacred wood of the Rowan-ash which the king is always seen to be carrying, is the true symbol of the Sun-worshipping Goths, Aryans or Sumerians.

Nowhere in the Old Testament is there any mention of honoring the Cross. Not until we get into the New Testament when St. John the Baptist is seen with his pre-Christian Sun-Cross of the Gothic cult of baptism (p. 67, *British Edda*) do we see the Cross. The uplifting and civilization of man had begun.

The Founding of Adam Thor's Capital

Sunk Beach, is benamed,
The fourth of the Inns,
Where the cool swelling waves
Are ever o'er clashing,
There Od(-am)-o'-the-Inn and his sages
Drink day after day,
Glad-hearted from golden jars.

We see in this lay that Adam Thor has built four centers of his empire named the Reign of Reason. This one, the fourth, is by the sea. We see Adam Thor with his eleven sages, drinking wine day after day, glad hearted.

This has a symbolic meaning, it doesn't mean that Adam Thor and his sages were drunkards. What it does mean is that their planning, civilizing, educating, enlightening, and their administration of just rule had the same effect on man as would the drinking of wine, gladdening the spirit and lightening the heart. Love is wine for the spirit.

Adam Thor Introduces Agriculture

Ād(-am) Bur's sons uplifted
The soil in cultivation.
They gave the Middle Garden
Its glorious merrie shape.
The Sun then cast its shine
Into the stone cellars (e'en in Eden).
The ground became green
With leeks (and) grain.

Fig. 8—Adam Thor or Dar as Lord of Agriculture bestowing Wheat plants and the Plough on his Gothic husbandmen. From a Sumerian seal of about 3000 B.C. Note the horned hats and the primitive Plough. (After *British Edda*, L.A. Waddell.)

Fig. 9—Aryan Cassi (Goth) colonists in tropical Babylonia ploughing and sowing under The Sign of the Cross, emblem of The Sun. From a Cassi official seal of about 1350 B.C. (After *British Edda*, L.A. Waddell.)

The Aryan's introduced farming. Adam was known as the Gardiner Goth, cultivating cereal grains of which there are no known original varieties from which these grains were developed into what we know today. They must have been native only to the lost continents.

Horses, cattle, sheep, goats and all the animals we find with man today were domesticated at that time, as none since of any consequence have been added to the list.

This holds true with the myth of Noah and the Ark although I doubt very much if Noah actually saved two of every kind by taking them into the Ark. It does, however, record the fact that the effort was made to preserve enough seed stock with which to start the new world.

> The sun cast its shine
> Into the stone cellars (e'en in Eden).

This doesn't mean the literal sun shining into the cellars as the sun rose and set over Eden before Adam's arrival the same as after his arrival. What it does mean is that the sunshine represents knowledge and enlightenment. The Edenities leared how to farm, thus elevating them from a day to day existence near starvation to a farming community of plenty, thus accrediting Adam with the feeding of the multitudes.

Institution of Laws and Industries

> Then go the Regi rulers all
> To their judgment stools,
> These great holy Goths
> And counselt together that:
> To the Night and New Moon
> They'd give these names.
> Morning also they named
> And mid day too,
> Dinner and afternoon
> The time for to tell

It appears here that the education of the Edenites had started, learning to tell the time and seasons by the position and phases of the heavenly bodies.

The Iron Age had already begun, Adam was already pounding out iron plow shears on his anvil.

Flaming forges and
A wealth of Smithies
Tongs too they shaped
And workmans tools
On tables in the town
They played cheerily in houses
Naught wanted they, nor gold

There is also mention of the Iron Age in Gen 4:22 "And Zil'lah, she also bare Tu'bal-cain, an instructor of every artificer in brass and iron."

Tu-Bal-Cain equates with the second king, King Cain himself. Tu-Bal means in Sumerian "The slayer of Bal (or Abel)" and with the affix "Cain" the identity with Cain is beyond dispute (page 298, *British Edda*).

SCENE III
CIVILIZATION OF ABORIGINAL DWARFS AND EDENITES
BY ADAM THOR

The first lay is reflecting back to the condition of the aboriginals before the coming of the Goths.

Until there came forth
Our suchlike lissome people,
Asas afill'd with love
In their happy homes,
There were found on the land
Little helpless mannikins,
Ash-smeared, howling, blue(-legged)
And fate-less.
Soul had they none, nor lineage,
Nor wit, nor headmen,
Nor crafts, nor letters,
Nor e'en a glint of God.
Soul gave them Od(-am) o' the Inn,
Wits gave them Hoeni,
Crafts gave them Löd Urr (Tubal Cain)
And the light of God.

Then go the Regi (rulers) all
To their judgment stools
The great holy Goths
And counselt together that:
"How shall we shield the dwarfs
And shape them into people,
Both from Brimis' blood
And from the Blue-Legs"?

In the last verse we see the holy Goths counselling together to decide how best to look after and protect these little people of the Lion tribe. How to shape them into a nation of people, a mixture of Brim's blood which is Wodans descendants and from the Blue-Legs.

Fig. 10—King Thor civilizing the aborigines of the Lion and Wolf totem tribes. From Hittite seal. *c.* 2300 B.C. Note King doubled for symmetry, stands under the Rowan-ash pedestalled Sun-Cross, which is winged, with a Hawk flying underneath, and lifts up by the hand a dwarf, whose companion is being attacked by a lion. Above are two tamed lions (or wolves) reconciled under the rayed Sun quadruped. (After *British Edda*, L.A. Waddell.)

As the aboriginal people of the Lion tribe became regenerated, they elected Chiefs among their tribes. The most regenerated of the Chiefs were then elected into the Gothic Parliament and were taught the art of government so they could rule themselves under the guidance of Adam Thor's empire. It has always been the policy of the Aryan race to subdue, uplift, educate and teach them how to form just government and then turn their rule back to them. The Aryans were the light of the world bringing hope to man.

The aboriginal people slowly became aware of a better way of life. The effect of the Aryan's civilization was making vast improvements in their lives, the regeneration of man was evident.

The Aryans taught them the civil code, established law and introduced the one God concept symbolized by the sun. The sun, being the sustainer of all life, was worshipped as the symbol of God and the outward manifestation of their worship was expressed by giving offerings of the fruits of the soil and the labour of their hands. In this way they abolished the cruel human and animal sacrifices of the Edenites.

They were taught trades and crafts, building and farming as they developed and became more educated. They were elected into the Aryan Government where they learned the skills of organizing people and decimating the law in a fair and just manner. As they qualified, self-rule was granted to them under King Adam Thor's empire, known as the Reign of Reason. The name of Adam's empire has the ring of freedom, making the subjects free moral agents. It provided man with the chance to use his God given ability to think and reason, to be in control of his destiny. Provided he stays within the guidelines of the law and the moral code he will develop to his ultimate potential, as opposed to the rule of tyranny a harsh unyielding law leading to suppression and regimentation of man, stifling his quest for knowledge and retarding his growth.

The Aryan's referred to the aborigine's as dwarfs, not dwarfs as stunted, but as small people. I wonder, could the pygmy tribes of darkest Africa be aboriginal people of creation, lost from the rest of the world in the jungles, undiscovered until recently?

From the semitic point of view the Aryans were giants which holds true with King James Gen. 6:4 "Giants were on the earth in those days."

SCENE IV
REGENERATED ABORIGINAL CHIEFS OF THE LION TRIBE
MARRIAGE WITH GOTHS

After a time when the Aborigines of the Lion tribe became civilized and educated Adam-Thor permitted inter-marriage of the select elite aborigines with Gothic maidens.

The inter-marriage of the elite with the Aryans and inter-breeding of the Matriarch, Edenites with the aboriginals would account for the varied races of today and a more uniform size of frame.

Thor and the All-Wise Dwarf

Dwarf Chief to his men quothes:
Broider the benches!
Now shall my bride with me
Hasten home together!
I'm in a mighty hurry (for marriage), everyone maun think.
But there's no resting now in squalid home for me!
       [He repairs to Thor in the Inn.]
Thor to Dwarf:
What is this, fellow? Why art thou so pale about the nose?
Wast thee dwelling o'ernights with corpses?
A likeness to the dour dunces (of Eden), methinks hangs
   o'er thee;
Thou wast not born (of the breed) for a (Gothic) bride!

D: All-Wise I'm named. I bide far aneath the earth (in cave);
Under the rock-stones is my homestead.
A wakeful man with witness am I come (to fetch my bride),
Let non unbraid this anguished foster(-brother).

T: I have the (wisht-for) bride in ward like a father.
I was not at home when the word-troth was plighted,
I who hallow the weddings of the Goths.
Winged Thor I'm called. Wide have I wandered,
Son am I of a civilized green branch.
Never without my will shalt thou have that young maid,
Nor get that gift-match from the Goths.

D: I will surely have to satisfy thee
To get that gift-match,
For (my life) I would liefer (sooner) hold in my arms than
   lack
That milk-white maiden.

T: The maiden's love thou maunna (mustn't) lack if thou
   (prove) worthy,
Wise guest and wooer: if thou
canst tell of every (land)

All that I wish to wit.
Say to me All-Wise all thou reckon'st of divers people,
Various, O Dwarf, that I (may test) thy wit!
How is the *Earth* hight (named) that lies before the sons of
　　men,
In every hame?

D:　"Ioerth" is it hight 'mong (Gothic) men, but "Field" by the
　　Asas;
"Way" it is called by the Vans, "Igreen" by the Edenites;
"Ground" by the elfs, and "Aur" 'tis called by the Regi
　　rulers.

　　(This is repeated with many other common names
　　　　concluding with:)

T:　How is *Ale* hight, as drunk by the sons of men,
In every hame?

D:　"Ale" 'tis called 'mong (Gothic) men, and "Beer" among
　　the Asas,
"Voice-giver" 'tis called by the Vans, "Rinse-lees" by the
　　Edenites,
"Mead" by the helots, "Assembly-drink" 'tis called by
　　young
Sutt's sons (Seth or Abel's sons)

　　(Thor satisfied, then bestows his consent to the match, with
his blessing in the following words:)

T:　In one breast, I never saw
More foreign word-staves!
Mickle tales (wisely) hast thou told, quoth I.
Of the Upper Class art thou, O Dwarf!
An umpire chief before thy day,
Now let the Sun shine into thy (dark) cellar (home)!
　　　　　　　　　Know ye yet the Edda?
　　　　　　　　　Know ye yet it all?

We see in this poem Thor giving his consent to the inter-
marrying of the Goths with the elite aborigines of the Lion tribe,
I would presume as there are numerous accounts of Adam Thor
taming the lions. It seems that this tribe more readily adapted to
civilization and I would venture to say that Abraham was the Chief
of the Lion tribe.

This poem also substantiates Gen. 6:2 "That the sons of God
saw the daughters of men that they *were* fair; and they took them
wives of all which they chose."

The Lion tribe, with the influence of the Aryan up-breeding in
their ancestry, became the American, British, Jewish and some
north European peoples. The tribe of the Wolf totem no doubt
became the Latin or Roman race, supported by the legend of
Romulus and Remus the founders of Rome who were suckled by
a she-wolf. The Serpent tribe could very easily be the peoples of
the far east as serpents and dragons play a major role in their
culture.

Although the people were becoming more enlightened, civilization was spreading, and the lives of the people were being
elevated to higher planes there was still an emnity towards the
white Aryan race, the Friend of Man. A jealousy and envy, ever
nurtured by the fears and superstitions which the Matriarch El
had so successfully implanted in their minds. We are no different
today, the same poisons of jealousy, vanity, and envy enter our
minds fostered by fear, superstition and ignorance.

There is one more point in this poem to ponder:

Thor says he wasn't home when the dwarf proposed to the
Gothic maiden. He says, "Winged Thor I'm called. Wide have I
wandered. Son am I of a civilized green branch." Now, just where
might Thor have gone? It appears that wherever he went it was
by air on wings.

If Adam Thor was the first God King of this Earth and he
introduced civilization to this Earth, where was the civilization
whom he was a son of? Proverbs 30 might give us a clue as to
where he went. Old Testament, Pro. 30:3 "I neither learned wisdom, nor have the knowledge of the holy. Who hath ascended up

into heaven, or descended . . . what *is* his name, and what *is* his
son's name, . . . ?"
Surely you know!

SCENE V
HOAR-BEARD

Thor is disclosed on a fishing expedition foraging out eastward
the prose prologue states and is stranded at a ferry over the sound.
What is he fishing for with no boat, fish or men? He hails the
ferryman (Hoar-Beard) across the sound.

These ancient dramatic Eddas also couched in a somewhat
"Shakespearan" style, nevertheless *existed in their present form
in MS. at least over five centuries before Shakespeare. (British Edda,*
page 36.)

Hoar-Beard's Tale

Thor and the Edenite Wolf-chief Hoar-Beard, disguised as a
Ferryman, have an argument across the sound.

Thor: Who is that swain of swains who stands across the
        sound?
HB: Who is that churl of churls who calls across the waves?
Thor: Ferry me across the sound, and I'll feed thee for
        to-morrow!
        I've a basket on my back with never better meat;
        I ate of it awhile afore I forged here from home:
        On Silder fish and heifer, and I'm still sated.
HB: An early worker boasting thy worthy meal thou art!
        Wittest thou clearly afore
        That drooping is thy home kin? Dead methinks is thy
        mother!
Thor: That thou sayist now is the very worst thought to me:
        That my mother is dead.
HB: Tush! Thou seem'st not a true Goth!
        Bare-boned thou standest and hast a beggar's garb,
        Thou hast not even thy breeches on!

Thor: Steer thou hither that oaken (bark), I know the
landing-place here.
Who owns the skiff thou holdest on that shore?

HB: Battle-Wolf is his name, he lives in Rādsey Sound
byre . . .
Say thou thy name if thou would'st cross the sound!

Thor: Must I tell my name? I am the outlaw'd to thy folk, Siag
(Sig or Sag),
With all our Oedls (Aethls) I'm a "son" of Od's Inn,
The bold Goth of Thrud (Troad). 'Tis with Thor the
Aryan Doomer that thou speakest.
Now will I ask what thou art named?

HB: Hoar-Beard I'm hight. Hide my name I never! But
E'en tho' I were no outlaw of thee, and were owner (of
the bark),
I'd keep my life safe this side the ford from such as thee,
Unless I was fair death-fated.

Thor: Harmful lout, were I to wade the waves to reach thee
'Twould wet my day's meal;
But I should pay thee (skin) swaddled swain for thy
mocking, could I cross.

HB: Here stand I and bide thy coming! . . .
I was in the army herd that went hither to thy workshops,
Bearing the war-banner and redd'ning the spear.

Thor: Now I get it from thee, villain! 'Twas thou that bade
those bannermen harm us!

HB: Beat thee yet shall I by a ring of spears,
When I'll be even with thee. Spears only will bring a
settlement! . . .

Thor: Where did'st thou learn such defying words?

HB: I learnt them at the mouths of the old robbers
Who bide in the hame howes (of Eden).

Thor: Thou giv'st too good a name to ditches
In calling them hame howes. . . .
Hoar-Beard, thou coward! How long hast thou delay'd
me!

HB: Get thee far from the sound! Thy passage is denied!

Thor: Then wilt thou now tell me the way (by land), since
    thou'lt not ferry me?

HB: 'Tis no long way to fare:
    A stound to the gorge-stocks, another to the stones,
    Then keep on the left till you come to Were(-wolf) Land.
    There may Fiorgn (the phrygian) meet Thor her son,
    And she may tell thee the forest-track to Wodan's Land.

Thor: Thou sparrest with nothing but mocking.
    I'll pay thee back for denying me passage if we two meet
    anon.

HB: Get thee afar now! May all the Grami wolf-fiends have
    thee!

This scene again has very little historic value if taken at face
value. But we can pick up our story thread if we look a little
deeper.

Thor is calling from his homeland across the sound to Eden.
Hoar-Beard answers him. Thor says, "If you like or if you let us,
we will come across the sound to Eden and will teach you how to
farm so you will have food for tomorrow. We have plenty, we will
share it with you and teach you how to cultivate the land." Hoar-
Beard answers with a little envy in his voice. He says, "You are
just boasting, you are a sad and sorry lot over there. I don't believe
you, you just want what we have got." Hoar-Beard asks what his
name is. Thor reluctantly tells him who he is, knowing that the
Edenites consider him their enemy.

Hoar-Beard knowing only their own treacherous nature, can't
understand anyone helping anyone out of compassion and concern. So, not trusting Thor, he says, "The only way we can rid
ourselves of your menace is by war." (This seems to be a part in
which history definitely does repeat itself since we see this same
thing happening today in Nicaragua.)

Thor pleads with him and asks if there is anyway he can get
across to them; his intentions are only to help, teach, and uplift
them. Hoar-Beard tells him to get lost!

In the next lay the Weaver of Thrud, Wodan, puts on a disguise
and goes over to Goth Land to spy on Adam Thor. He wants to

see how they live and learn their secrets of success. This is no different from espionage which is continually employed among the nations today.

Wodan quoths: "Far afield have I fared, much am I tempted (to fare): I will fox out the Regi rulers.
Thither will I hie, and wit how The Weaver of Thrud's
Home and kindred stand."
(Wodan goes on to tell his many disguises.)

Grim, the Hooded Serpent, we're named and Gangrel,
Harrier (Old Harry) and Horror-bearer,
Thekk, Thrid, Thut and Uth,
Sadr (Saturn), Hell-blinder and Hoary
Warrior-father, Nick o'Night (Old Nick).
All-father, Val's father, Around-rider and Sea-farer.
Bileyg, Bale maker and Manifold Sorcerer:
By one name ne'er am I named,
Since I forked forth amongst folk.

Grim am I hight, when against George-the-Red (Adam Thor)
And Jalk against Āsmun Dar,
But Kiala when I drink from the chalice (grail of Eden). Vidur in
the fights, Oski and Ōmi,
Gōndlir and Hoar-Beard with the Goths,
Swithur and Svidr was I hight at Scyth Mīmi's,
When I deluded them at the inn—(this) old Edenite:
I the Mid-wolf valiant, to the merrie sons of the Inn
Became their one bane.
Wodan now I'm named, Ogn was I afore,
Thunder was I named afore that,
Gaut and Gelding with the Goths,
Ovener and Sooth-Serpent: these words I ween.
All come from mine own self.

What we learn from this lay is something that we no doubt know—that Satan comes in all manners of disguises, deceiving us, appearing in the most unexpected places, at the most unexpected times, beguiling us and leading us into temptation. Rev. 12:9— . . . that old serpent, called the Devil, and Satan, which deceiveth the whole world: . . .

As the poem goes on, Wodan enters Adam Thors hall or inn, claiming to be a humble Edenite thirsting after knowledge. Adam Thor interviews him. During the interview Adam Thor asks him questions concerning the Aryan beliefs. Wodan answers with all the right answers. Then Wodan has his turn at questioning Adam Thor. Although this seems to be corrupt, according to its anachronism the questions which Wodan asks deal mainly with Thor's future battles with the Edenites, and the successor to the Gothic Kingdom, and the outcome of the future events.

Wodan:	Which of the wise Asas shall rule the Goths When Surt(ar)'s fire is slacked (in Eden)?
Thor:	Mōdi (Thor) and Magni shall have the hammer (sceptre) After Wing's (Thor's) last fight.
Wodan:	What shall become of Od-o'-the-Inn (Thor), In his old age on the ripping up of the rulers?
Thor:	The Wolf (Loki, Baldr or Abel) maun gulp at the Old Father (Ad-am Thor). Then maun Vidar (Thor's son) wreck the Wolf, He maun cleave its cold jaws, When a witness at the fight.

Know ye yet the Edda?
Know ye yet it all?

Of course this last verse parallels the end time prophecies of the Bible.

SCENE VI
CONQUEST OF PHRYGIA BY KING ADAM THOR

In this scene we see Adam Thor taming the lions. This has been recorded on many prehistoric monuments of Cappadocia and Phrygia. Taming the lions is symbolic of Adam Thor's civilizing the aboriginal tribes of the Lion totem. The name "Phrygia" is a

Sumerian word for Asia Minor. It means land of the lions and at that time it was under the dominion of the matriarch of Eden, El or Frigia.

Adam Thor was successful in his conquest; as we see in the "Prose Edda" it is recorded in these words—

"The sons of Hek Tor (Adam Thor) come to Frigia Land and established themselves in that land. But banished Elanus, whom the Asas call Ale (El).

Wodans Lament on his Rout in Phrygia by Thor Meide-Asa (Midas) or George with his Red Cross.

"I see against me Hekk (Adam Thor) Meide at Vind
Who in the night with all his nine (wood crosses),
He, Geire (George) wounded me, giving it to Wodan:
To myself to mine own self.
With these (woods) of Meide, of which no man witted,
  Everyone of them routed me, and I ran!

That living wood shielded me not, that wood without
  horns! Those nine standards I feel aneath.
Seized by the upstanding Rowans, with weeping seized,
I fell away, back from them.

There must be a significance to the nine Rowan-ash crosses which Adam Thor used to banish the devil worshipping Edenites from Phrygia. Maybe it takes one Rowan-ash cross to banish one each of the nine heads of the Hydra. This could very well be the origin of the practice of exorcism.

It appears that this battle may not have been a battle of weapons, but the triumph of love, truth, hope and knowledge over suppression, deception, fear and ignorance.

A unique specimen of prehistoric fine art was found in Egypt in the year 1914. It is believed to be the ivory handle of Adam Thor's own hunting knife, a magnificently carved record of Adam Thor's conquest of Phrygia. On it is a contemporary carving of Adam Thor taming the lions. It was proven by M. Benedite, through it's art, to be non-Egyptian and considerably earlier than

Fig. 11—Midas Monument in Phrygia with its Nine St. George's Crosses *c.* 1000 B.C. (After *British Edda,* L.A. Waddell.)

the first Dynasty of Egypt and presumably brought as a trophy from Mesopotamia or Syria, (Syria was an early name for Asia Minor). These conclusions were fully confirmed by Sir Flanders Petrie who considers it the oldest and finest object of high art from the known ancient world, and dates it to before 5546 B.C. This date is based, however, on the "long" extravagantly early conjectured date of Menes who I find by new historical evidence, reigned about 2703/2641 B.C., or six centuries after Adam Thor, whose real date is about 3380/3350 B.C. (page 47, *British Edda.*)

These dates being established, could it not be possible that this ivory handle could have originated in Atlantis and recorded the conquest of Phrygia as one of Adam Thor's expeditions for colonizing and civilizing the aboriginal tribes under the domain of the Matriarch El around the shores of the Mediterranean Sea?

Adam Thor was succeeding in his civilization and uplifting of man. Man was learning to live together in a peaceful, civilized manner. Along with civilization comes education, laws were es-

Fig. 12—Thor or Dar conquering, taming or civilizing the Lion-totem tribes of Phrygia and Asia Minor and Chaldea, from carved ivory handle of knife *c.* 3350 B.C. (After *British Edda*, L.A. Waddell.)

tablished for the good of all, schools and colleges were established, everyone received an education, knowledge was expanding at a fast rate. There was no reason for it to be otherwise as King Adam Thor had come from the seat of all knowledge and he freely decimated to all who were willing to learn.

We can assume this is Adam Thor, under the title of Fish or Fisher King, in the legends of every race being teacher of writing and agriculture and teacher of all wisdom. In China, Fu-Hi, the keeper of the mystic tablets containing the mysteries of heaven and earth is pictured as having a fish tail.

What powers they used and along what line they developed is not available for us to determine. They could have harnessed the forces of the cosmos in ways which we have not yet comprehended. The molecular structure of matter was the same in those days as it is today, however, and the laws of science and the laws of nature which were set in motion from the beginning have not changed, so it is quite reasonable to believe that their knowledge

KING THOR TAMING OR CIVILIZING THE LION-WOLF
TRIBES OF PHYRGIA.

Fig. 13—Ivory handle showing tribal combatants in human form. Note below two types of boats with Goat-head emblems on prow. (After *British Edda*, L.A. Waddell.)

and civilization progressed along similar lines as ours today. The Creators, by having advanced knowledge, may have bypassed the automobile and concentrated on air travel, thus making the vast networks of highways unnecessary.

SCENE VII
THOR'S CAPITAL CITIES

At this point we will return to Plato's account of the kingdoms in Atlantis rather than continue with Thor's capital in Cappadocia at Vidara in Pteria. Later we will see Adam Thor with his capitals in Cappadocia, Asia Minor and Palestine. At this point Adam doesn't have a son so Cain is not even in the picture yet. Adam has only built eleven inns or cities and there are only ten Asas besides Adam Thor who makes the eleventh. The twelfth of course is Abel-Sut or Loki (or Satan) and his capital is in Eden, named Vall-Hall. Cain will become the thirteenth Asa to take the place of the twelfth, the fallen Asa Abel-Sutt.

'Heaven's Burg' is the quarter
Where the Home Dale (Father now)
Quoths his bold (ethic) maxims.

There the warder of the Goths
Drinks with the house-holding husbands
The glad mead in the Inn of the Goths.

Adam Thor has now established marriage and the family unit with the husband as the head, as opposed to the Matriarch when promiscuity prevailed and no family unit existed, no lineage or family tree.

'Glittering' is the tenth Inn,
All studded with gold
And thatch'd with silver beseeming.
In it Foresight (Promētheus)
Bides flitting each day,
Soothing and settling all scathes.

New-town is the eleventh Inn
There Nioerd heaved himself
Up a carved hall,
He the peacemaker of men,
The bane of the base.
'Tis high timber'd on the Red Horn.

The Red Horn is the site of Adam Thor's upright planted Red Cross standard.

Thor's Judgment Hall

Thor gangs to the Judgment Inn (of Court)
And wades the rivers.
The Körmt and Örmt
And the two Kerlaugs,
There shallows Thor wades
Every day when he fares to Doom Inn,
At the Ash of Ygg's Dra-sill.
For the (road by the) Asa's Bridge
Burns all aglow (below)
Where the holy waters hulloaing flow
But (a-horse) on Glad and Gill,
Clear and Race-Fire,
Silver-Tuft and Sinew,
Surety and Pale-Hoof,
Gold-Tuft and Light-foot,
The other (ten) Asas ride there (by the bridge)
Everyday they fare forth to the Doom Inn
At the Ash of Ygg's Dra-sill.

This establishes the number of Asas in Thor's court, ten plus Adam, eleven all told. I mentioned that all the legendary and mythical figures stem from only six individuals, there of course may be some who represent the ten Asas, but I cannot define which ones.

Fig. 14—Thor or Ygg's Drasil Ash guarded by Deer (Dar). From Hittite seal, *c.* 2000 B.C. Note it grows on mountain (Mountain Ash or Rowan) and its fruit seen in twig below is like a rowan. (After *British Edda*, L.A. Waddell.)

Fig. 15—Thor, Dar, or Ygg's Tree from Babylonian seal, *c.* 2000 B.C. The inscription records that owner was votary of Sun-god *Asur (i.e., Ahura* or Asaru title of In-Dara or Thor in Sumerian). (After *British Edda*, L.A. Waddell.)

The Tree of Life

The Ash I see standing;
'This hight Ygg's Drasill,
Highly beamed oozing
Whitey aureate (apples).

Thence come the dew drops
That fall in this dale.
It stands aye afar from
The green pine of Urd Burn (of Eden).

Three roots of it stand out
At the three highways
Under the Ash of Ygg's Drasill.
To Hell-Byre (Eden) goes one
Another to the rimey frost-giants (of Ararat)
The third to the baptized men
Of men (the Goths at Vidare town).

Harts too there are four,
Their heads thrown up, who
With (long) necked Geese gnaw (its boughs);
Dainn and Dwalinn
Are they named and
Duneyr and Dyrathror.

The Ash, Ygg's Drasill,
Drees more distress
Than men have witted of:
Harts bite it above,
At it sides it rots,
And the Nether-ogre shears its aneath.

Hear we have the legendary tree of life with light oozing out all over, bright like gold with its rowen apples. All the good things come from it like the dew drops in the dale. It's a far cry from the pine of Eden which they have to decorate to try to make it shine. Adam Thor offers it freely to the Edenites and aborignal man and to the Goths. The Goths are the only ones that feed on it, aboriginal man ignores it, leaves its fruit to rot. The Edenites undermine it, hack at its roots and try to destroy it.

Thor as Bil the Baptist

Five hundred floor (-steps)
And forty pairs of tow-ropes (hand-rails).
Me thinks (lead up) to Bill-the-Baptist's with bays.
The house there
Its raftered, I wit,
Small, I see, yet most mighty.

Water baptism is unknown among the Semites and in the Old Testament. The practise of baptism was re-introduced by John the Baptist in the beginning of the New Testament. John the Baptist appears to be, as portrayed in art, with his pre-Christian Sun-Cross and his practise of baptism, to be a devotee of the pagan Sun Cult of Adam Thor. A revival and return to the original and true religion introduced by Adam Thor of a monalithic God represented by the Rowan-ash Cross, or the Fine Cross, or the pre-

Fig. 16—Thor or Dar (In-Dara) as "Bil-the-Baptist," with Life-giving Scouring Waters. From Sumerian seal of Gothic King Gudia, about 2370 B.C. Note the horned Gothic head-dress, and costumes of that period, with long beard and shaven upper lip. The fruit-bud on the top of vase is the Sumerian word-sign for "Life." (After *British Edda*, L.A. Waddell.)

Fig. 17—Thor or Ad(-am) as Atum, the Egyptian father Sun-god, baptizing the infant crown-prince. From sculpture at Luxor. Note he is in Hawk-headed as well as human form. This purifying water is called in the inscription "Water of Life and Good Fortune, rejuvenating thee like thy father Atum." (After *British Edda*, L.A. Waddell.)

Christian Cross of the Sun Cult, as opposed to the Matriarch devil worshipping cult of the moon or darkness, represented by serpents and wolves and requiring cruel sanguin animal, and even human, sacrifices.

Fig. 18—St. John the Baptist with his pre-Christian Cross-standard or Sun-mace of the Gothic cult of Baptism. (After *British Edda,* L.A. Waddell.)

It appears that baptism was the initiation rite into Adam Thor's higher religions, represented by the Sun-Cross. That the New Testament Christianity was an attempt by the Aryan, the devout Sun-worshippers, including the Sumerians or Goths, to return the world; by means of their crusade, undefiled by the Mother-Son cult of Eden; to the ancient pagan Sun-Cult.

I am not suggesting that the Old Testament is not inspired writings, but it has been influenced by El, and if the right of baptism was practised in that time, which it no doubt was, it was reduced to daily bathing and washing for hygienic purposes.

SCENE VIII

VISIT OF EVE AND OTHER AMAZON WEIRDS (VALKYRS) OF EDEN TO ADAM THOR'S CAPITAL

Mother El of Eden; bitterly jealous of Adam Thor's civilization, the rule of reason, his advancement in education, and the standard of living of the Goths and the aborigines of the Lion tribe whom he had civilized; sends her Amazon Weirds to spy on them. This scene and the next is the origin of our nursery rhyme story of Cinderella. The evil step-mother is the Matriarch El, the two ugly stepsisters are the Fate Weirds of Eden, and Cinderella is Eve who eventually marries the handsome Prince Adam Thor.

It appears that Eden was a Matriarch society as opposed to Adam Thor's patriachal society with the introduction of marriage and the family unit. Women were dominant over men, there was no marriage or family life, promiscuity was accepted, children were raised in day care centres and by babysitters, and there was no family life. There was little knowledge of lineage, if any it was traced through the female. I am not painting a picture of an extremely evil people with women clad in skins, brandishing spears and massacring the Goths. By this time, through their spying on the Goths, they had developed a civilization, but it was based on material gain, greed, and vanity.

If you examine our society today you can see we have a tendency towards the same thing. Our society is based on material gain and vanity and if you notice through the woman's liberation movement we are showing a tendency towards a return of a matriarch society. We are seeing a bigger share of the important decisions in business and politics being made by women, we are seeing more children raised by day care centres and babysitters and more single parents raising children, thus losing the family unit. We see women demonstrating, demanding the right to deny life to their own unborn babies. We see more promiscuity all the

time. We even see a turnabout in the home, mothers having the
babies and mothers earning the wages while fathers stay home
taking care of the house. He is neither the bearer of children, nor
the winner of bread. Where is all this leading?

I am definitely not denying women the right to express themselves but not at the expense of their children, the next generation,
our most valuable resource.

> She (Ymi) wotteth of the Home-Dalers,
> List'ning to the folk
> Under the Hawk-banners
> And holy-beam'd tree.
> She sees them oozing with
> Torrents of good cheer
> In pledging the Valiant Father.
> > *Know ye yet the Edda?*
> > *Know ye yet it all?*

> Then came there less Mary's maids,
> Giant (Amazon) maidens
> Much vexing over runners
> From their hame in Eden.

> I see these Valkyrs of Ior
> On a visit up-coming,
> Geared for their riding
> To great Goth people.

> Skuld held a shield
> And Skogul another,
> Gunn-Hilda (Eve) and Göndul
> And Geir Skogul.

> Now are they all told,
> The nuns a-visiting the Aryans
> Geared for their riding
> Go the prying Valkyrs o' Ior.
> > *Know ye yet the Edda?*
> > *Know ye yet it all?*

SCENE IX
EVE'S COURTSHIP AND MARRIAGE WITH KING ADAM THOR

Eve as Freyia, quoth;
>Waken, Mary May, maid. Waken my wench!
>O Hound-sister, who dwell'st in Hell's Byre!
>Now is the time for a rake of rakes! Let's ride with the
>>skulkers (wolves)
>To Vall Hall, and thence to holy Vès (Vidara).

>Let's beg the Aryan Father to seat and hug us!
>For he gives geldings and hunting hawk-spurs to his
>>bodyguard,
>He gave to Her Modi a helmet and breastplate,
>And Sig the minor got a sword (Excalibur?).
>He gives victory to his 'sons' and gold ore to some,
>Speech-skill to many, and manliness to his men.
>Byres he gives to his breek'd men, and songs to the bards.
>He gives an honourable man to many an upright (maid).

>Thor maun I worship, and thus maun I beg him:
>That he aye be at peace with thee—
>Tho' he is no friend with the brothel brides of Eden:

>Now take thy wolf from its stall,
>Let him run with my Rowan!
>Slowly my colt will trot on the Way of the Goths.
>I will saddle my mare of mettle.

Heide, El or Mary as The Houndel:
>False art thou, Freyia,
>>and tempting me!
>'Tis that wise thine eyes and mouth (now) turn!
>Is't that thou hast thy choice steed (Rowan) from
>Ottar-of-the-Inn, Inn-stone's young Bur?

Eve:
>Deluded art thou, Houndel, and surely dreaming,
>To say that my husband (to be)
>Has to do with this choice comrade (steed),

That is the glorious colt Gold Bristle,
Hilda's swift charger, hedge-reared me
By the dwarfs twain, Dainn and Nabhi.

Let's chat from our saddles, seated with the wolf pack,
But be just to the race of the Doomer (Adam),
The groomsmen who come from the Goths.

They have wagered (for my hand) in choice gold meal
    (dust):
Young Ottar-of-the-Inn and thy sweetheart son Ty (Baldr).
But I shall grant that young Skati of the Inn
Has a father's heritage after our friendship.

He built me an altar of piled up stones,
And rubb'd their grit smooth like glass,
And redden'd it (for me) with new nout's blood:
Ottar has aye been true to Asyn of Ior!

Now let's hear again the pedigree tale
Of the upper-born race of men!
Who were the Shield-ings? Who were the Skilled-ings?

Who were the Edl-ings? Who were the (mere) Yelp-ings?
Who were the Born Land-Holders? Who were the Aryans
    born?
The most chosen men in Mid-Gard?

(Here Heidi or Gul recites the genealogy of Adam's
    forbears as again repeated to Adam Thor himself later,
    as we shall see.)

Eve:

Bear thou all these bound in thy mind to bark them out,
So that he all these worthy words will pick up
Readily on the third morning hence,
When he and thy sweetheart son Ty, their races will
    reckon.

Hound:

Sniff away on the trot hence thyself! I list after my sofa.
Few fair words of friendship shalt thou force from me:

Galloping after thy lover Adal, out at nights
Meeting the He-Goats (Goths)! Fare away thou Heid-of-
the-Rowan (Apple)!

Running after Ödi, ever yearning,
Scuttling off there in skirts still more.
Gallop thyself, O Edl's lover! Not to-night (shall I)!
Thou'rt the same as these farmer folk. Fare away thyself
Heid-of-the-Rowan (Apple)!

Eve:

I'll slay thee, fiery Eldi, tho' thou be Ivi's old mother.
If thou com'st not hence on the road!

Hound:

Here quench thy burning ire! Hold thy flame!
Wert to happen that (he) lose his life, it could be thol'd.
Bear thou to Ottar's hand this beer,
Blended with adder's drops and ill-health of Hell!

Eve:

Thy weird Hell spells shall work no harm (on him),
As thou think'st, O brothel bride of Eden! Nor thy baleful
curse.
He shall drink Dyr's (Dar's) own wine,
And I shall ask Ottar and all the Goths for doughty
support.

We notice in Scene IX that Eve invited the Matriarch Mary May, or El, to accompany her to Adam Thor's holy city, Vedara, and to her wedding. The Matriarch declined, she wouldn't leave her fortress in the East; however, Abel-Sutt was in love with Eve too. Adam Thor and Abel-Sutt were both wooing Eve. Abel-Sutt escorted her to her wedding hoping he could still win her hand and return to his Mother and Eden with her.

Now we see the Matriarch, that old Serpent, in her fortress in the East, ready to come running to her lover-son when he is wounded and slain by Cain. Not in love and compassion as Aphridite came running to her wounded lover Adonis, but in all fury and vengeance as is seen in Scene XXIV, the Battle of Eden and Adam's subsequent victory.

Apparently at the time when the Matriarch El took the authority from the God of Heaven and took over the rulership of Earth she recruited followers from some of the other kingdoms of the creators as disclosed in this verse.

> Sunder'd born much, I think,
> Are the Norns (Nuns of Eden)
> Their race is not the same.
> Some are rear'd of Asa kin,
> Some are rear'd of Elf kin
> Some are daughters of the Dvalin Dwarfs

Her Gothic or Asa race is confirmed by an ancient seal of about 2000 B.C. in Metropolitan Museum, New York (p 72, Fig. 56, *British Edda*).

Fig. 19—Eve or Gunn (Guen-Ever) as priestess of The Bowl of Eden before her marriage with Adam Her Thor. From Babylonian seal of about 2000 B.C. in Metropolitan Mus., N.Y. (After *British Edda*, L.A. Waddell.)

In a lovers quarrel from the Indian Vedas, the sacred books of the Eastern branch of the Aryans, Eve discloses the true nature of the Edenite women.

Eve: I have gone from thee like the first of Dawns.
Parū of the Sun return to thy home:
I, like the wind, am difficult to capture. . . .
Go home again, thou fool;
Thou has not won me!

Para (Adam Thor):
> Thy lover shall flee forth this day forever, to seek,
>   without return the furthest distance.
> Then let his bed lie in destruction's bosom,
>   and there let fierce rapacious wolves devour him.

Eve: Nay, do not die, Purū, of the Sun,
> Non vanish; let not the evil omened wolves devour thee!
> With women there can be no lasting friendship:
> Hearts of hyenas are the hearts of women!

You notice that Eve refers to the Edenite women as having hearts of hyenas. Hyenas are a matriarch society, the females are dominant over the males. We must realize that in this symbolism that woman equates with the church or congregation, the congregation is mankind, so however Eve acts toward Adam Thor, or woman towards her husband, is mirroring the way mankind is acting toward his God. When a matriarch society is expressed it means that mankind is trying to become dominant over God. Or at least independent of God (a Godless society).

But it also expresses the fact that women are gaining an understanding of the mundane workings of this world and business, which has been in the hands of men up to the recent past. It also shows that mankind is gaining a better understanding of the workings of this world and the cosmos which has hither to been in the hands of God only.

It appears that the scriptures, the Edda's, and all the ancient classical literature has the same basic theme, it's a love story. With God represented in the masculine gender as a lover wooing a beautiful maiden which is mankind, but within the human race there is still another division, male and female which we can see to demonstrate the plan of God.

When God woos a person and wins the love of that individual and that person, man or woman, submits to God, it is consummated as likened to the sexual act between man and woman after marriage with the subsequent conception of a new life. With God submission of an individual to the love of God is consummated by the imbueing or impregnating of that person with his holy spirit, creating a new spiritual life, the inner man.

These love stories all follow the same theme. The churches of this world, the congregations being mankind, represent the betrothed maiden who has been flirting with Satan unfaithful to God. God, with the help of his first born son St. Michael or Cain, is trying to win her back.

This may have something to do with the misconstrued idea as held by men in the past and especially the old Jewish belief that women were less than men, with no souls and considered as chattels of men. Men played God, Lord, and master over women practising polygamy and making love to whom they pleased and it was considered natural, women bore the brunt by being labelled sinners and harlots.

The marriage of Adam and Eve is recorded in the Indian Vedas and Epics in the Sanskrit form as "Paru of the Sun" and Asi of Ur (Unu-asi).

"Now, in the days of yore, the nymph Aru-Asi dwelt with the royal seer Puru-ranas; and having made a contract with him, she lived in wedlock with him." (Page 230, *British Edda*).

The marriage of Adam and Eve is also recorded in a Greek poem by Aeschyles as Pro Metheus; i.e., Bar Mioth of the Eddas and Hesione, as recalled by Oceanos.

> "What divine strain I sang thee then,
> Around the bridal chamber,
> And around the bridal bath,
> When thou my sister fair, Hesione,
> Won by rich, gifts dids't lead
> From Ocean's caves thy spousal bed to share!"
> (Page 231, *British Edda*)

Genesis version of Adam and Eve's marriage in Hebrew Genesis we read:

"And Adam said 'This is now bone of my bone and flesh of my flesh. She shall be called Ash because she was taken out of Aish. Therefore shall Aish leave his father and mother and shall cleave unto his wife and they shall be one flesh . . .' And Adam called his wife's name Eve (Gen 2:23–24 and 3:20).

Here it is seen, on comparing the Hebrew text with our English Authorized and Revised versions, that the later Hebrews and our

English translators of this Hebrew text have made the personal names or titles of Adam (Ad-am) and Aish—the latter from the Aryan Sumerian A's, title of Lord Dar, and his Eddic title Asa or Lord, and of Eve or Ash from the Sumerian title of A's on Ash or Azu for Dar's wife into generic terms for "man" and "woman" by equating them to the Semitic Chaldee Ishu and Ishshu respectively; and thus effectually disguising the old personal titles in the Hebrew text tradition. Ivi, which is Adam's wife's name in the Edda as well as in the Hebrew text, is rendered as "Eve" in our English verses. (Page 229, *British Edda.*)

From rock sculptures at Iasili near Pteria of about 3000 B.C. we see the wedding procession of King Adam-Thor and Eve (Page 81, *British Edda*). Eve's wedding procession is described in the following verses.

Eve's Wedding Procession to Adam Thor's Capital, with Her "Brother" Abel or Baldr

Rodes Baorg (Baldr) to the burg, the battle-frothed son of Wodan,
Frey (Eve) also on her first of battle-steeds Gold Bristle.
That choice rider (Eve), of the kin of the sea-foam,
gallops to the hearth of the Goth.
That Raven-priestess (Eve) a-horse is much fallen in
with the Home-Daler (Father Adam).

But rides with ill-will on his Fraeg (wolf) as a little mare,
The ruffian Ty (Bladr), gaping, the murd'rous mauler, the baleful son.
Their hags of the rune secrets of victory, the swift-swilling Valkyrs of Ur follow,
For their 'holy' blood sacrifice (riding) on Ravens. To draw blood lots are they so minded.

Let the preceding verses speak for themselves, they seem to be in keeping with the rock sculptures at Iasili, describing the wedding procession in detail.

The two (Adam and Eve) are seen exchanging a cross-like emblem which is surmounted by a globe, which I have shown to

MARRIAGE CEREMONY OF ADAM-THOR & EVE

Fig. 20—Marriage of King Adam-Thor and Eve with Wedding Procession. From rock-sculptures at Iasili near Pteria of about (?) 3000 B.C. Note Adam in Gothic garb carrying his mace, borne shoulder-high by his men and attended by his royal Unicorn Goat, meets Eve, who is also given the Unicorn as his betrothed queen, and both bear an apple-like symbol. Eve is followed by the Edenite Baldr or Abel; both mounted on cat-like lions or leopards. Loki, Bal, Bul, or Baldr bears a double axe, which in Sumerian is *Bal,* with the definition "The hostile lord Lockh," *i.e.,* Loki. Behind him are the Eden weirds, mounted on a two-headed vulture. The retinue of Adam or Her-Thor, carved, like himself, nearly life-size on the side of the rock sanctuary, are here omitted for want of space. (After *British Edda,* L.A. Waddell.)

be a Rowan Apple of Ygg's Drasill Tree of Knowledge, and emblematic of the Red Sun-Cross of St. George, somewhat like a "Celtic Cross"; and Adam's Gothic wood cross was made of this Ash tree. This Rowan Apple is now seen to have been the source of the perverted Jewish legend of Eve tempting Adam with the apple which was to the Edenites, under the Matriarch El of Hell, 'The Forbidden Fruit" as it symbolized Adam's rival cult of the Sun and God and Heaven. Abel, as Baldr or Loki, bearing the double axe, which in Sumerian has the name of Bal, is thus clearly identified and confirmed by the name being defined as "The hostile Lord Lukh," i.e. Loki. (Page 80, *British Edda*.)

Adam introduced marriage as part of his higher civilization and uplifting of man as opposed to the pre-Adamite period of the Edenites where promiscuity prevailed.

We have seen in this poem that Ty (Abel Baldr); Eve's stepbrother only in so much as Eve was the adopted priestess daughter of El, the Mother of Ty; Ty and Adam were both suitors after Eve's hand in marriage. Symbolically we must remember that the Church or religious cults are referred to as women, so he who won Eve's hand had won the religion and she would be faithful and worship him only, so symbolically both Abel and Adam were contending for the rulership of this world.

We also see that Ty (or Abel) is referred to as the Matriarch's sweetheart son, thus establishing their identity with the serpent worshipping mother and son cult of the Romish Church. We also see that Eve calls the Matriarch El, Mary May Maid.

Quote from Page 305, *British Edda*—"Meyiar means maids or virgins, singular Maer which is a frequent title of the Matriarch and also used in later Christian times in Iceland and Norway for the Virgin Mary (Page 443 *Icelandic/English Dictionary*. G. Vigfusson. 1874)."

Eve, after her spying expeditions into Goth Land as an Amazon priestess of the serpent worshipping cult of the Matriarch El, realizes that Adam's way, the way of the Aryan civilization, was the right way. She renounced her priestesscraft in the serpent worshipping cult of Eden.

On repentance Eve was forgiven of her past sins and was baptised in the "Water of Life and Good Fortune" as an initiation into the Sun-worshipping cult of the Aryans, thus becoming the She Goat, the mother of the Aryan Race. Establishing the teaching of the New Testament of repentance, baptism, and the forgiveness of sins.

At this point it is very interesting to note the parallels between the events and circumstances surrounding Eve's life. That she was of Aryan race, the same blood as Adam; that she chose to become a priestess of the serpent cult of this world and later denounced it and chose to wed Adam, who later was deified as son of God, over Abel (or Loki), who later became Satan, who was also wooing her. She bore a son to Adam Thor whom she named Cain, who later was deified as St. Michael, the Archangel, the Son of the Sun God.

As compared with the ancient historical records concerning the Virgin Mary, her life and the birth of Jesus Christ, Mary was born to a high priest of the temple of Helios or Temple of the Sun at the outer gates of Jerusalem. Mary was pledged to the temple at birth, when she was three years old she voluntarily stayed in the temple and became a vestal priestess of the temple. At the age of almost thirteen she had the choice of either staying on in the temple or leaving the temple in the care of a widower by the name of Joseph, but not to become his wife. She was then impregnated by God and bore a son Jesus, who later was deified as the Son of God. After which she married Joseph and bore children to him, which is worth noting as we will discover later. It is remarkable to notice that Joseph was said to be a carpenter, thus making him the owner of an axe which equates him with Loki (or Abel) in the rock sculpture of the wedding procession. Mary's genealogy is traced back in the scriptures to King David and on to Adam and God comparable with that of Eve's genealogy. According to the Gospel of the birth of Mary, "The name Mary was given the child by command of the Angel." If it was pre-ordained that she was to be named Mary, there must have been a reason, which I will endeavor to explain later. It is also interesting to note that in Roman Catholicism the month of May is consecrated to the Virgin Mary.

In pre-Christian Rome the month of May was dedicated to Flora, the Goddess of Spring, i.e. the Matriarch Mary May Maid which was celebrated in lycentious gaiety on the first day of May.

Does this make the Temple of Helios, the temple of the Sun, into the temple of Satan! I don't think so, this too is symbolic. The temple used here is represented by all twelve tribes of Israel, it is used symbolically for the temples of Rome.

SCENE X
BIRTH AND BOYHOOD OF ADAM THOR'S SON
GUNN KON OR "CAIN" OR "GAWAIN"

King's son and hetman hero
Kon was the youngest (Asa) i' the Inn,
As up he waxed as an Earl born,
He learnt horse-taming, to fend by shields,
Shafts to shape and shake ashen spears.

Kon-the-Young kent the Rowan Runes,
Eve's Runes and the olden Runes, too.
Merrily he kent how to save men's lives,
Sword edges to deave and bring foes down, did Aegi.

He learnt the clack o'(wild) fowls, and how to quench
    fire,
Sores to assuage and sorrow to allay,
Able in energy, he equalled eight men.
Rode Kon-the-Young through scrub and shaw,
Fledging his golf-club and quieting the fowls.

He as Earl with Rig the Runes doled out,
But beat him in poetry which he better knew.
Then getting the Aedl-dish (of king) he got into his own,
And Rig (King) was he known, the Rune-kenner.

Seated there (at Vidara) on a how
And slogging his harp
Was the jigging herder of the king's men,
The gladsome Egid (Aegi),

His spurr'd hunting hawk-hen
Above him in a wooden cage,
The red Fag falcon-hen
That's hight Fialar (the Fowler).

Here we see Cain as being well-educated and well-rounded in all skills, especially in the knowledge of science and of the ancient mysteries. He saves men's lives and is far superior to normal men, he was well able to express himself in vague poetic form or in parables and he was called King even before his time of kingship.

All these astounding facts which parallel the life of Jesus with the life of Cain are undeniable. Line for line comparison, there can be no mistake Jesus's life is a re-enactment of the original Son of the Sun-god.

Kon the Young, knew the Rowan Runes, Jesus knew the mysteries of the (Rowan), the symbol of the Gothic Cross, the pre-Christian Sun-Cross. Jesus is not referring to the profane cross of the later Christian period where he is portrayed as beaten and nailed to the cross, nor is he at that time referring to the cross in anticipation of his crucifixion. He is referring to the so called pagan cross of the Sun Cult, the only true religion as seen in Matthew 10:38 "and he who does not take his cross and follow me is not worthy of me."

"Sores to assuage and sorrow to allay," Jesus healed the sick and alleviated the suffering of man.

"Able in energy, he equalled eight men." Jesus unquestionably was far superior to any man or number of men. If we were to look for Cain in his personified form today we would have to look for him in a body of men, not just one man, like an organization, ministry or brotherhood. The Sun hero Conn, the fighter of a hundred, expresses the same thought. We have an interesting fact in the next two lines:

He as Earl with Rig the Runes doled out,
But beat him in poetry which he better knew.

Here Jesus; as an Earl, Prince, or heir to a future kingdom; was brought before King Herrod and Priests, but more interesting yet, he gave them answers in poetic form which they were unable to understand as is evident in Christ's teaching in parable form of which only the elect could understand and is evident in the Eddas. The poetic form in which it is written has remained a mystery for thousands of years and eventually disregarded as a source of history, was labeled myth and legend of the Christian era. This also applies to the manner in which the scriptures are written.

One more line which equates with Christ: "And Rig (King) was he known, the Rune-Kenner." Jesus was called the "King of the Jews" before his time.

(His Summerian reigning title of Azag, discloses him as a Harpist and sporting falconer, is described in the Indian King-List as the original of Nimrod and bears in Sumerian the title of Nimmirud (page 89, *British Edda*).

Aryan Kings possess many names, titles and aliases—personal, ancestral, territorial, regional and religious—just as Hommer gives many different titles for his leading heroes. It has been proven by L.A. Waddell that names and titles which apply to Cain, among others, are—Aegis, Azag, Bauge, Bacchus, Maku, Michael, St. Michael, Dionysas, Thiaze, Lo-the-Rider, Gawain, Kon, Horus, Qain, The son Duke, Gan-esna as Lord of Grain and Wealth and in Homer as Erichthonias.

By tracing our Kings, heroes and Gods by their titles and names back through our many varied legends and myths we can see all nations have a common ancestry in the aboriginal man of creation with the influence of the Matriarch El and the Edenites, in rebellion to the laws of creation that are required to maintain and nourish the creation and bring it to fruition on the one hand. The influence of King Adam Thor and his Aryan or Gothic race, the Sons of God, who teach obedience to the spiritual laws which enable man to live together in peace and harmony, combining their efforts, expanding in knowledge, elevating themselves to higher planes of comprehension, and unveiling the mysteries of life and the universe, so the very purpose of our life will be made known, and the uncomprehensible will be comprehensible and we will be one with God. Only then will we realize the purpose of this life.

CHAPTER 5

The Creation of Myths and Legends

It would be vanity indeed for modern man to presume that he alone, in all time from the beginning, from Antediluvian time to this present day, has acquired the sum total of around ninety percent of all knowledge in a mere one hundred years. From the horse drawn era to inter-planetary space travel. We are now re-learning the knowledge our ancestors possessed before the great destruction, the flood of the Old Testament. This knowledge has been preserved in fragmented pieces, scant recollections and mere germs of ideas from 3380 years B.C. by the keepers of the secrets of the Mountain Stone or Holy Grail, faithfully and religiously guarding the secrets and dispensing them at the allotted times for the advancement of mankind.

History has a habit of repeating itself, it revolves in cycles, it goes around and around as we saw in Ecclesiastes, "there is nothing new under the sun." If we don't heed the lessons of the past and get in stride with the laws of the cosmos, the same will happen to this era as happened to the civilization before us.

To get a better understanding of the past we should turn to our wealth of myths and legends, our heroes and Gods of the ancient past. Their tales of deeds to their epic making heroes carried from mouth to ear from the previous civilization through the great destruction, or flood, to this era. We must put ourselves in the

70

shoes of the story tellers and through each successive generation of the promulgators of the tales of their ancestors.

For an example of the birth of a legend we could simulate a condition very much the same as a remnant of the survivors of a holocaust would be in.

Suppose, this isn't possible in this day and age, but just suppose a jet airliner carrying some two hundred or more passengers, men and women from all walks of life, was crossing the Pacific Ocean, ran out of fuel, and had to make a forced landing in the ocean about a half mile from the shores of an uninhabited island, luckily making a soft landing and no one was hurt, but the plane was starting to sink. The passengers managed to escape the sinking plane, casting off excess clothing and any personal possessions they may have had with them to lighten themselves for the long swim to shore and survival.

On reaching the land they found an abundance of fruit, wild animals of different species, and schools of fish in the water around the coast of the island. All that was needed to support life was in abundance, the climate was warm. There was little they needed to survive. They could fashion crude tools from the stones or from wood or bones. The coconut palm afforded them the necessary clothing.

After awhile they adapted to life on the island and set about the job of living and making the best of it, and the raising of children began.

Their favorite pasttime, which became a sort of ritual, was to sit around the campfires at night and reminisce of the old days back in America with all the pleasures and gadgets of modern day life. They would tell their children about automobiles, television, skyscrapers, airplanes, pop and ice cream.

They tried to explain the workings of things but the children had a hard time understanding, even with a fertile imagination, that which they had never seen or experienced. Even a simple thing such as ice—water so hard you can walk on it—when they had never even experienced cold!

Under these conditions it is possible to give birth to a legend of an ancient God. It could start like this . . .

The parents would tell of times when relaxing in the evenings they would listen to the radio, they would listen to the news and to the President. When he spoke to the nation they would tell the children that he was the Commander-in-Chief. They would also tell them how they liked to listen to their favorite stars. The children would ask questions like, "Do you mean the stars in the sky?" The parents would answer that the stars they were talking about were real, famous people. The children would ask, "How could you hear them?" The parents responded by saying that their voices would be sent out around the country by electrical power and could be heard everywhere at the same time by everybody. In time all the old original people would have died, and the elders of the next generation would carry on the ritual of telling the stories their parents told them. This would go on from generation to generation with each successive generation comprehending less of the reality of the story. They would have to make it tangible, something they could associate with, so the story of the radio could become thunder being the voice of the stars talking to them sent with the great electrical power of the lightning. The descendants of these marooned civilized people would have degenerated into primitive people by this time. They would be retrogressing instead of progressing; completely opposite from our modern day conception. They would even think they had forgotten their mother tongue, this would be the reason for not understanding what the thunder was telling them, they would be fearful and give offerings to appease it. They would develop the art of fashioning stone into spear heads, arrowheads, axes, bowls and other tools. They would become quite adept and skillful at utilizing what the island had to offer. By chance they may have found some free gold in the streams and found it could be melted in their stone bowls and fashioned into tools more efficient than their stone tools. The slow process of advancement would have begun. They would have developed a culture unique to themselves with further development of their culture and the skills of utilizing the resources the island had to offer. They would look back on the unskillfully made stone tools that they found in the ground around what they considered to be the old campsites of their ancient forefathers, the ones who were marooned on the island. In their vanity they would consider priding themselves on their advancement and skills, and discredit the stories of the radio as a mere myth invented by a simple people who didn't understand the causes of an electrical storm.

It seems quite plausible by the foregoing example of the birth of a legend that legends do not spring from the minds of the primitive by their observance of nature and the natural law which they have no control or power over, or would have any reason to believe they should have.

It is my belief however, that myths and legends arise from the rubble and ashes of previous civilizations brought to destruction by their own hands, or natural disasters. The few knowledgeable ones, without the means of reconstruction, relating the events and wonders of the bygone age to the new and rising generations. It is not until countless generations have passed and the slow process of civilization and advancement in knowledge has reached a point where man's imagination has broadened to a point where anything he conceives is possible, that he can look back if he is not prejudiced by his vanity and realizes that some of the mysterious things described in our myths and legends were actual accounts of happenings handed down by people who didn't fully understand them. Elijah's chariot of fire might have been an attempt to describe a rocket or aircraft of a civilization even more advanced than ours today. Fal's fiery stone wheel or Typhon's sun chariot; which in mythology he lost control of and it scorched the earth, almost burning it up, until Thor struck it down into the sea with his mighty thunderbolt; could have been some type of nuclear missile employed in a great war bringing to a close the end of an era which has been recorded in our legends as the great flood.

There are other accounts of strange things recorded in our history and legends of ancient times confounding us still, as they confounded our forefathers.

If we look at Samuel 6:6–7—does this portray a loving, merciful, forgiving, just God?—"And when they came to the thrashing floor of Nacon, Uz'zan put out his hand to the Arc of God and took hold of it, for the oxen stumbled and the anger of the Lord was kindled against Uzzan; and God smote him there because he put forth his hand to the arc; and he died there beside the Arc of God.''

I would say this is an interpretation of an event which happened several hundred years earlier by priests who had lost their understanding of the truth and were relying on their own reasoning to record the facts of which I don't doubt their accuracy. Azzah no doubt was struck dead. Looking at this event through our twentieth century eyes, could it have possibly gone like this . . .

The Lord came down to Moses and gave him instructions to build an arc. This arc was an electrical condenser, fashioned on the same principle as a laden jar. The electrical power was required to power a transmitting and receiving radio which could be used for receiving instructions and for asking advice. The testimony which the Lord gave Moses to place in the arc could have been the radio. It would be the spoken word, the testimony of God.

Moses might have received instructions which went like this: "This is a highly charged, delicate piece of electrical equipment. Don't let anybody meddle with it. If anyone touches it that doesn't understand what they are doing they may get electrocuted." This was misinterpreted by the scribes and priests into any angry God smiting dead anyone who touched it, even in the act of protecting it.

Exodus 25:22 "There I will meet with you and from above the mercy seat, from between the two cherubim that are upon the arc of the testimony. I will speak with you of all that I will give you in commandments for the people of Israel.''

The history of all people start with a dynasty of God-kings. The Egyptians, British, American Indian, East Indian, Mexican— all nations can trace their beginnings back through the legends, traditions and deeds of their heaven-descended monarchs, all funneling back to King Adam Thor, his Queen Eve, and son Cain, or the Matriarch El and her consort Wodan, and Son Loki, Abel or Sutt. There are no other divine Kings, although in each tongue they are known by different names. They are the only human equivalents of the founders of all nations.

Do we have a legitimate reason to believe that a civilization greater than ours of today could not have existed prior to the flood when we have the mighty pyramids standing as silent witness, saluting the ancient past. The past where the very Gods of our creation, the source of all knowledge were their kings and teachers, all the secrets of the cosmos were known, all the laws of nature were know. This knowledge was decimated to the aboriginal man as he advanced to great heights of knowledge and civilization and in their vanity, claiming to be wise, rejected their creators and turned their knowledge of creation into instruments of destruction.

SCENE XI
CAIN'S FIRST COMBAT WITH BALDR OR ABEL OR "THE GREEN MAN," ADVERSARY OF SIR GAWAIN

Cain, waking up after the exhausting battle with the Edenite Baldr or Abel:

Gunn-Ar awaking from swoon, quoths:

"What is this beating burning (in my brow)? Why have I
    been sleeping?
Why is my felt (cloak) off me? And I pale and needy?"
He then swore:
"Sig-the-minor, Bur's son, shamefully slit (art thou) afar!
In the wretched Raven's Land, Wae's me, warrior of
    Sig-Ur-Dar!
Long have I slept, long have I slumbered,
Long have I lain low!
O Od-of-the-Inn, for thy weal I was not mighty (enough)
To brandish a blunt stave (spear)!"

This scene describes a battle between Cain and Abel. It is not a battle in the normally recognized sense, fought with swords or lances, as romantically portrayed in the Arthurian legends by such romancing Bards as Sir Thomas Malory in his *Le Morte D'Arthur,* and other such books. It was, rather, a battle of morals and principles, the ever present battle between good and evil.

Young King Cain, as he is referred to in the Edda as Sig-the-Minor (young King), just attaining manhood was the victim of a very subtle seduction by Abel. Symbolically Cain is standing on a hill looking south to the land of the Edenites. there he saw the glitter and glamour of the bright lights of Eden; they looked so inviting, interesting, and intriguing, he starts down the hill towards Eden and there he meets the Lewd Man (Abel).

Cain, on meeting Abel, was challenged. A mighty battle was fought. Abel fought with all his might for he knew if he could win this battle over this young king he would have won his whole kingdom.

Next we see Cain, not beaten though exhausted, waking up from a swoon reproaching himself for wandering so far from his own kingdom. He says, "Woe is me for being lured and tempted into the glitter of Eden, how long have my eyes been closed, how long have I been in Edenland? As we realize, the longer we stay in Edenland, the duller our sword becomes and the harder it is to fight our way out."

Although this may be a little obscure to some there is an obvious parallel here between Cain's first combat and Jesus's temptation in the Wilderness. Whereas Jesus, after his confrontation with Satan in the wilderness, was exhausted and was administered to by angels; Cain on the other hand was exhausted after his battle with Abel and was administered to by Eve. Then Eve goes on to explain the battle, stating that it was a battle between two kings on their border; one being Satan and the other being Cain. She also points out that Satan or Abel is older than Cain and the most quarrelsome.

It is of interest to note that Abel is older than Cain and not his younger brother as we already saw in the wedding procession. Abel was already a man before Cain was even born.

Gunn-Ar (Cain) quoths to Eve:

"Hail dawn! Hail days since!
Hail night and peaks!

Out of mine eyes, I see us two hither,
And seated giving sighs.
Hail Asas! Hail Asyn of Ior!
Hail! I see thy worth manifold in this field!
Tell and gift us with the merry man-wit too,
And may thy healing hands tend me all my life!''

She (Eve) adds the descriptive text, ''is named Sigrdr (fa) and was (formerly) a Valkyr. She said (reminding him):

Eve quoths:

''A fight between two kings on their borders.
One, the Hooded (Serpent-chief),
And the other the helmuted Gunn-Ar.
He that was the old one was the much vexer of the Inn
   (Baldr-Loki-Abel).
And the warrior of Od-o'-the-Inn, he is called Sigri
   (Little Sig):
Then the Hooded One baited his easy-going 'brother',
Who was a wight in the field quite willing to accept.''

Know ye yet the Edda?
Know ye yet it all?

Eve had been a former Valkyan or Amazon of Eden, a vestal priestess of the Matriarch El's serpent cult. On denouncing the demon religion of Hell to marry Adam; on repentance and baptism into Adam's Sun Cult where she assumed the capacity of high priestess; she became the dispenser of the fruit (apples) which she plucks from the sacred tree of life and feeds to the Aryan Goths. This qualifies her to administer to young Cain and heal his wounded conscience and nurse him back to moral strength, knowing well the subtle nature of Abel.

Symbolically the Church or religion is symbolized by a woman. Eve represents the body of the Church feeding, caring, and nurturing the spiritual man as compared with a physical mother, feeding, caring, and nurturing physical man.

SCENE XII
EVE IMPARTS KING ADAM'S TEN COMMANDMENTS TO GANN, CAIN OR GAWAIN

The Ten Commandments of Adam Thor on the Duty of Love

These commandments are basically the same ten commandments which Moses claims to have received from God on Mount Sinai with the exception of the fourth, the keeping of the Sabbath. As we see here the commandments were introduced by Adam Thor as part of his higher civilization and Solar Cult, almost two thousand years before Moses time and kept by the Aryan or Gothic people. As seen by Abram, a Semitic of the Lion tribe, paying homage or tythes to an Aryan King (or Hittite) of which he was a subject sharing in the benefits of their civilization. This king was Melchizadek, King of Salem or Urasalim. The sacred city of the Hittites later known as Jerusalem, sacred city of the Jews (Gen 14:18). Salem, according to my reasoning, was one of Adam Thor's walled capital cities.

Melchizadek, King of Salem, must have been one of the twelve Asas of Creation. The description of Melchizadek in Hebrews 7:3 "He is without Mother or Father Genealogy and has neither beginning of days or end of life but resembling the Son of God he continues a priest forever." To require a walled city he must have been on this earth in human form. If he has no end of life, where is he now? It is my opinion that all the ancient magnificent walled cities, the wonders of the ancient world, were built by our creators for protection from the savage raids of their creation while they were civilizing and educating them. As man became more civilized more was put under his jurisdiction and our creator Gods receded more and more into the background, eventually returning from where they came leaving the Chaldean and Semitic tribes or Kingdoms in control of their cities or, as in the case of the Israelites, turned Salem over to King David which later became the Sacred City of the Jews, Jerusalem. It has been conjectured by some denominations that Melchizadek was in fact Jesus the Word by which the world was created. John 1:1–3: "In the beginning was

the Word, and the Word was with God, and the Word was God.
He was in the beginning with God; all things were made through
him, and without him was not anything made that was made.'' Or
he could have been St. Michael (Cain). In Akkadian Melchizadek
is spelled Milki-ilu or Malchiel Accad (Akkad) originating from
Erech the original kingdom of Nimrod (Cain).

We are on the subject of the commandments and it is ques-
tionable as to whether the fourth, the Sabbath, did in fact exist
prior to Moses' time. It is still more extraordinary that the Jewish
Sabbath should be Saturday. Saturday means Saturn (Satan), but
maybe it was to identify them with Satan for the purpose of the
fulfillment in the order of things; to be the persecutors of Christ
which we will see later.

It is only logical to assume that Sunday would be the holy day
of the cult based on scientific sun religion in which the Lord of
the universe is specially identified with the great luminary, the
light of the world, on which day the remaining eleven tribes of
Israel cling to, from whom Christianity springs, and Jesus being
the light of the world.

Eve quoths: Hug Runes should'st thou knoe if thou would'st be
Gooder than the swains of common men.
Now shalt thou choose whether I be silent, or bid me
These whetted (moral) weapons launch at thee!
Saying these, or hearing them in silence, handcuffs thyself
  to Hug.
All are from the mind of Meti (Mioth, Mithra, Adam).

Gunn: Flinch not will I, e'en tho' I knew I was death-fated:
I was not born a coward blade.
Thy loving counsels all will I (cherished) keep,
So long as I shall live.

Eve: This I counsel thee *Firstly:* That thou with thy friends
Blameless be;
E'en tho' they heave sides against thee, scathe not in
  gore.
That will duly speak (for thee) when thou art dead.

This I counsel thee *Another:* That thou swear no oath
Unless thou know'st it to be true.
Grim limb'd goes the tricky ruffian,
A harmful wretch is the pledge-breaker.

This I counsel thee *Thirdly:* That thou in the Thing
    court
Deal not hardly against (witless) homeless helots.
For a witless mouth may let out words
Worse than it wots of.
Not all (confessions) are wanted. If thou against him
    'tush,'
He'll think thee midst the coward blades born,
Or, soon for settling it himself will say:

'Hated are the words of a homeless people,
Only the Goths get Justice!'
Then another day forth he'll fare
And launch himself against the (fancied) lissom liar.

This I counsel thee *Fourthly:* If a byre (Edenite)
    fortune-teller
Blameful be in the way,
Going on beyond is better than staying there,
E'en tho' night o'ertake thee.
Foresighted eyes are needed for our sons,
Where skulking wolf-wretches are in the way.
Oft where a baleful visaged woman stands near the
    beat(en track)
There's a sword deaver (Edenite) in the sedges.

This I counsel thee *Fifthly:* When thou see'st fair
Unwedded 'brides' (Edenite) on the benches, and
Silvery-tongued, let them not rid thee of sleep,
Touch not the women nor kiss them.

This I counsel thee *Sixthly:* Tho' high words fare forth
At Ale-banquet meets, still never
Deal scarlet drunk men with the doleful wood (sword).

Much wine steals the wits.
Jibing sayings over ale have hustl'd
Men to moody grievous wrath,
Some to baneful death, some to baleful staves:
Manifold are the griefs to their farers.

This I counsel thee *Seventhly:* If thou has a scathedeal
With a huggable men or helots,
'Tis better to brawl and burn outside,
Than inside with odious (word) staves.

This I counsel thee *Eightly:* That thou shalt see no ill,
And forego false speech.
Touch not a maid nor another man's wife,
Nor egg them on to shame.

This I counsel thee *Ninthly:* That thou an outcast save
Where'er thou findest one outside a fold.
Where there's a sick-dead, or sead-dead,
Or weapon-dead man,
Thou shalt lave and garb him, and lay him
Kempt and dried, ere in the kist he fares,
And bid him sweetly sleep.

This I counsel thee *Tenthly:* That thou ne'er trust
Pledged words o' a Wolf-triber a drop,
Where thou has baned his brother,
Or hast fell'd his father.
The Wolf remains in the young son,
Tho' he may have been gladden'd with gold.
Scathes and hates think not of even in sleep,
Nor hold them in thy arms.
But wits and weapons every one wants to fetch
When they fare forth midst foreign people.

Once again we find a parallel between Cain and Jesus. Cain
answers Eve, "Flinch not will I e'en tho' I knew I was death-
fated: . . ." Jesus also flinched not even though he knew he was
destined to be crucified for keeping the moral law.

Scene XIII
Adam Thor's Capital Attacked by the Edenites
of Van under Baldr or Abel

East sat she the Old One
In the Iarn (Cedar) Wood,
And fed the Fen Wolf's kin.
The warder of them all
Is the one knocker-down:
The Moon's (cult) Ti, the ogre
Of the troll fiend's skin.

He fills the four quarters
With fey death-fated men.
Riding o'er Reason's (Thor's) seat,
He reddens it in drops (of gore)
The sward becomes sunless
Until the summer after
Breaking all troth pledges.

Know ye yet the Edda?
Know ye yet it all?

Notice the old Matriarch is in the East, and there feeding her wolves. "Old Mother Hubbard feeding her doggies a bone."

Storming of Adam Thor's Burg

What is the holm mount hight,
Where shall blend in hurling battle
Surtr and the Asas together?

Ōsk-Ōp-ni is it hight,
Where all the skulking wolves
Shall fight the Goths of Geir (George).
Bil's roost bridge shall be broken.
As they (the Goths) forth fare
But they swim the muddy mere.

The Battle and After

Broken was the border wall
Of the Asas' burg:
The Vans knew craft enow
To break down the walls.
But Od(-am) o' the Inn flak'd (arrows) down
On the folk and scatter'd them.
That was the first folk-fight,
The first in the Himin home.

Then go the rulers all
To their rock-stools (in parliament);
The great holy Goths
And got counsel together:
Whether should the Asas
Yield to suffer loss,
Or should the Goths all
Get war-gild (from the Edenites)?

As we saw earlier, Adam Thor's system of education and civilization was progressing rapidly, as they were taught by their God, their very creator, as could be compared with the speed an underdeveloped third world nation could be developed by America today.

The Edenites, although hostile toward them, still sent their spies among them, consequently learning and advancing along similar lines, as we see in the verse entitled The Battle and After. The Vans knew crafts now, I am suggesting that they are in possession of some very sophisticated weapons.

SCENE XIV
AMAZONS AND THE FLOOD

Thor quoths:

I was then in the East
And guarding the river,

When there set on me
The sons of the Swearer (Wodan).
With grit they 'barded me,
Yet gain'd they no victory:
Tho' so wordy, yet had they
To beg their freedom from me.

Wax thou not now Vimur!
For methinks I'll wade thy tide
To the Garden of Eden!
If thou wish'd to wax,
Then I'll wax all my Asa might
Even as high as heaven!

Once in thy company
Needed I my Asa might
In the Garden of Eden.
Then Yelp and Grip were dinted
By George-the-Red,
Tho' they wish'd to heave me (back) to heaven.
Thor quoths:
The bear-sark'd brides (of Eden),
I battled at Hlēseyio (Layas).
They worked the worst wounds,
And welted all the people.

She wolves were they,
But scarcely women.
They scaled my ship
Which I had shored,
Hack'd me with an iron club
And chased young Thia (-assi or Cain).

> *Know ye yet the Edda?*
> *Know ye yet it all?*

Scene XIV is more of the same. Jealousy, envy, and hatred were embedded deep in the hearts of the Edenites. Not unlike today, small underdeveloped nations which America and Britain are accused of the crime of feeding, educating, financing, and civilizing. When they are half-civilized they turn on their benefactors and call them names and accuse them of exploiting them. There are wars all around us, of course these scenes of war on Adam Thor's boundaries equates with Jesus's prophecy in Matthew 24:6 "and you will hear of wars and rumors of wars; see that you are not alarmed for this must take place but the end is not yet, for nations will rise against nations and kingdoms against kingdoms."

In the last verse it appears to be a return to matriarchy in that time before the flood, or destruction; as it appears there is a trend toward matriarchy in this era before the end time. Slowly and subtly, but surely, these things creep up on us; first the women suffragette, which seems right; then comes the women's liberation movement. Who is it that is whispering in our mothers ears, telling them that feeding, forming, guiding, loving, caring and shaping the next generation is least important. Who will be our rulers in our old age? Is it not a worthwhile job to be mother and housewife, as compared to awaiting table, answering the phone, being on an assembly line in some factory, or being president of a corporation?

I do not wish to be thought of as a male chauvinist and because of that I would like to take this time to explain that all life; plant, animal, and even human; require that the female egg is fertilized by the male sperm of life to continue life. Even Mother Nature requires the rays of the Sun to generate life. Life on Earth is like a female egg; if it is not fertilized by the spirit of our Creator, referred to in the male gender "our Father," it will have but a short life and will die.

When a matriarchate is expressed I mean that when El usurped the control of this planet from Adam Thor and the Lord's of Creation she was cut off from them. She took for a consort a created aboriginal, Wodan, and begot a son; Loki, Abel, or Satan, meaning that he is of this world, for this world and by this world only; thus putting mankind in the female gender, a matriarchate. If mankind were to live in this world under the Eden triad it would end up in self-destruction. In order to live under a patriarchy we must accept our Creator and be impregnated by him. Then life will continue and we will become Gods ourselves eventually.

Isiah 3:12 "My people, children are their oppressors and women rule over them. Oh my people, your leaders mislead you and confuse the course of your path."

The bear-sark'd brides of Eden, the Amazons of Eden, had a hand in the binding of Pro-Methius as surely as the women of today are helping to bind those who have the responsibility of leading the nations today.

A woman liberationer, when interviewed on television, having changed her opinions in her new book on sex was referred to as a disillusioned warrior. The modern Amazons are out in force gaining momentum as time shortens, demonstrating for equal rights, not satisfied with being women and not only wanting equal rights with men, they want to be treated like men; in fact they want to act like men. With their anti-nuclear demonstrations, ban the bomb demonstrations, and peace marches in the same breath they demand the right to murder their unborn babies. It's quite a paradox and thus they deprive themselves of the greatest love affair of their life.

It appears with this new wave of abortion, demanding women want control over their own bodies, she ignores the feelings of the man whose baby she is carrying. This is yet another reflection of mankinds reaction to his God. Man is advancing in knowledge, becoming more sophisticated in his thinking. He is teaching evolution, that there is no God, that he is master of his own destiny, in complete control, thus aborting the spirit of God, answerable only to himself.

The Combat

Reason-Jogger o' the Inn (Thor) turned the raging stallion
    (Baldr) at Singa Stane.
The famed one o' the Wood (-Cross) turned the foul, sly,
    fearsome Bauta's (Wodan's) wary son:
That mud-flinging boaster did the son of the Sea-Pearl
    mother (Thor) fag out,
Whose one family thought, I ken, was Adr's murder.

Drawing nigh with a heavy tooth'd tang, a ruddy-biting
   tang,
Killing by the runes of his queen Ninna (El) tied to an
   ell-long (tool),
That raider was risking counter woe from his 'brother,'
   Mag's father (Thor).

Then came to the brow of honour'd Endr (Andara) the
   barbed one, the murderer flung
Till his own son (Cain) swerv'd it by the Reg's sword
   silently out o' the rift.

Next I see him (Thor), the hated o' the Edenites, alight
   on Sooty (Seth)—
Hell's son o' the Harpy o' the grit howes, Una o' the
   bangle,
Ok (Thor) against Iarn Earth's wolf-son, when down
   (came he):
Mod (Thor), the cool Meila's brother (lit) on Moony
   returning to his hens.

(Meantime) the almightly batsman Ullar (Cain) ended his
   own log for the match,
For the ground was graped by the rain o'burning (stones)
   of Ginnung woe.
Then the helmeted Regi o' the He-Goat guards (Cain)
   rode softly from the track,
Warily agog, the widow Svol-ni's (El's) son, the Ruiner,
   for to find.

Turning off from Baldr's border berg-folk, those scathing
   devils,
Yet wishful to barge on the braggart, that lover of Rān
   (El), the 'heavenly' Moony,
Miaok (Michael) was not far ahint Moet (Thor), in that
   strip o' Murky Wood,
Where lying down, he wit the fight atween his daring
   father and that bane.

Brisk flowed the barges that bound Ollo's gaze on the
rounds.
Shy under his shield, ill and icy for his father's good
against the Dīsi.
For the warder's (Thor's) hack from his hurter, the rugged
young hero (Cain) waited not long:
The hammer's snout on that troll o' the runes tidily fell
and bit.

The breath-spiller (mace) let fall on Fial's brow, on that
yelling ox's brow—
On that baleful young warder, Belia's Bull—rent his helm,
Then kneed he the ground, that guilty Gram (wolf) afore
the sharp hammer,
When Dana o' the Bergs beat and broke tht Iaormun, the
traitor.
Then the hard broken chip o' the Harrier (Baldr) found a
hame in Thing Odar of Ving.
When that horn hit into his roof-bone and grounded the
swain,
There in Od o' the Inn unloosened, buried in his head,
That steely spike stood sticking fast in Einrid's blood.

Afterwards out it was niggl'd by Gefion's son Ale (Cain)
from the sore,
Ty's red iron-ore was got rid of, the Hell-ball was quell'd.

The wounding of Adam Thor is an extremely important time
in our history. So much so that all ancients have recorded the
event in their legends in its many differing forms, which makes it
obvious to the reader of the many varied accounts that it has a
subtler meaning than the obvious.

The fact that Adam Thor was wounded by Abel-Sutt lobbing
a piece of iron ore at him and lodging it in his head, wounding
him, would have been recorded as such with no mystery attached.
But, as in all the Eddic poems, there is a symbolic meaning of
which I will endeavor to explain.

Fig. 21—Adam Sig, *Zax* or "Zeus" attacked by Typho (Tivo or Abel-Seth). (From altar frieze of Pergamon.) Note Thor or Sig with his bolt or hammer, attended by his Eagle or Sun-Hawk, overthrowing Tivo (Baldr-Abel), whose legs end in two Serpents and who is heaving a huge stone. In left-hand border young Cain under his shield watching the contest as described in the Edda. (After *British Edda*, L.A. Waddell.)

This event records a great battle between Adam Thor and Abel-Seth or between good and evil, or God and Satan. In the Greek version, the legend of Pro-Metheus Bound, depicts a time in history after Adam has successfully repelled the attacks of the Edenites on his borders as shown in the last two scenes. On failing to conquer Adam Thor's empire by force, Abel resorted to subversive means, infiltrating into his empire. Abel worked within Adam's borders, blinding the eyes of the people with the glitter of materialistic things, wealth, and a general selfish attitude of the way of "get" rather than the way of "give."

The wounding of Adam is also referred to as the long lob, symbolizing that Abel-Sutt had managed to wound Adam from his capital of Eden by remote subversive tactics.

Adam Thor was fast losing his influence on man. With the knowledge acquired by man from Adam Thor's system of education, civilization and listening to Abel's agents who were among them, they became vain. Listening to their own reasoning, they rejected Adam Thor's way, consequently adopting the ways of Abel and the Edenites which inevitably leads to corruption. This constituted the symbolic wounding of Adam Thor. Being wounded in the head symbolized his loss of control of his empire. We must remember that Adam was only wounded, not dead—this is very important.

How long they remained a Godless nation I don't know, but Cain set about nursing his father, Adam, back to health. How this was done will be explained later.

Abel divided the people of Atlantis, who were Adam's kingdom, against themselves; having no God, and no direction, there was confusion. Abel, having stolen the secrets of science from the Atlantians, started to amass an arsenal of nuclear missiles to destroy his arch enemy once and for all. The people of Atlantis, choosing to live the way of the Edenites, but in peace, saw that war and annihilation would be inevitable. They turned on Adam and their Aryan leaders, condemning them as evil for the crime of befriending and being the champion of mankind, teaching and increasing their knowledge. As the legend has it, they accused him of the crime of being the best friend and champion of mankind and stealing fire from heaven. It is thought by mythologists that the fire he stole from heaven was the introduction of fire to the hearth, which it was not as reference was made to the cooks fire in Scene I. "The savory breath of sooty black loiters o'er the cooks fire."

The fire he is accused of stealing from heaven was the knowledge of science he dispensed leading to the splitting of the atom and the weapons of their destruction.

In deeming themselves to be wise they became fools. Condemning their king and Aryan leaders as evil, claiming themselves to be righteous, they demanded he be tried in court before the God of this world (Satan) and he was sentenced to be staked to a rock in purgatory for eternity.

The Atlantians, claiming to be righteous, sought the way to peace by stopping the advancement of knowledge and not maintaining their lead over the Edenites, which was playing right into Abel's hands. Seizing the opportunity the Edenites launched an attack on Atlantis which resulted in the sinking of Atlantis and the continent of Lemure, subsequently flooding the rest of the world.

Even before the destruction of Atlantis Satan spread the word that Adam was dead and the world believed him. Now Adam was thought to be dead by all the world, except by Cain and his Aryans which only amounted to a few in comparison with the population. Cain, next in succession, assumes the throne of Adam Thor; making Cain a king before his time. Adam Thor is now recovered and continues to remain with Cain in an advisory capacity for another one hundred and twenty years. Gen. 6:3—"My spirit shall not always strive with man yet his days shall be a hundred and twenty years."

If we refer to *The Makers of Civilization,* page 482, we see Cain rules in both the first and second dynasty. The first dynasty, I suggest, was before the flood on the continent of Atlantis, or rather the war of destruction. Surviving the war he set up his second dynasty in Mesopotamia from which time we have accurate historical records.

The sinking of Atlantis and Lemuria may not have been impossible, as one might imagine. It has been the opinion of those who have proposed the theory of these continents that before the underground gas belt had formed, encircling the earth, Atlantis and Lemuria were sitting on a honey-comb of vast gas pockets which would be ruptured by the explosions of war, adding fury to the inferno, causing them to collapse and consequently the sinking of the continent. This would result in tidal waves, inundating the remaining land masses, leaving devastation in their wake, resulting in the geological proof of the flood as we see it today. Water levels would no doubt remain higher, submerging forever the sites of the old cities which were on the coast. The salt water would rust and oxidize any remaining evidence that was made of iron.

Adam Thor and Cain had the foresight to see the inevitable. Preparing for it, they moved to safety enough seed stock in the way of domesticated animals, cereal grains, cultivated fruit trees and vegetable seeds; just the bare necessities to start rebuilding the world anew. This corresponds with the Old Testament account of Noah and the Ark.

This is no doubt the origin of the mythical Gods; Adonis, Attis, and Osiris; worshipped by the remnant of the tribes that survived. Adam Thor, thought to be dead, was resurrected and deified God, and regenerated new life on earth.

It signifies the destruction, desolation of the world and near death of the world and its regeneration by Adam. The dates are also significant, the re-birth of the world with the new Sun on December 25th and March 27th, three days after the date of the destruction, symbolizing new hope with the bursting forth of spring, as was worshipped by the remnant of humanity. The survivors of the destruction came running back to their God as Aphrodite came running back to Adonis when he was wounded. The pine tree, the sacred tree of the serpent worshipping matriarch cult of Eden, was a solemn reminder of who crucified their God. If, as we have been lead to believe, that God destroyed the world because it was wicked, why then does man celebrate the Death and Resurrection of God? God would be very much alive, it would be the world and man that would have to be resurrected.

To let the mind wander for a moment, I wonder if in the Genesis account of Noah his three sons and their wives would in fact represent symbolically Adam Thor and Eve as the Father God, his son Cain and his wife, Abel-Seth and El, and aboriginal man and wife. The good, the bad and the created.

There are many legends which support the account of the flood from all parts of the world so we can rest assured that there was a disaster of that magnitude in our history.

If the disaster had been of natural causes there would be no pointing finger or accusations.

The most common account is the biblical account of Noah. There is also the Greek legend of Pyrrah and Deucalion. Zeus is inclined to destroy Earth by fire, thunder bolts and lightning, but later changes his mind for fear of burning up Earth's axis, and floods it instead. Pyrrha and Deucalion were the sole survivors, they created man by throwing stones over their shoulder; page 84, J. E. Zimmerman, *Dictionary of Classical Mythology* states "The flood sent by Zeus at the end of the Iron Age;" page 429, Larousse, *Wold Mythology,* "Accounts of the flood have been found among Samoyed, Vogul and Ostiak tribes. They refer to a tidal wave of water or fire which covered all habitable lands, man and their animals escaped by taking to boats and they waited on mountain tops for the waters or flames to recede."

There is the legend of Ty stealing his father's sun chariot, at which time he lost control of the horses and came too close to Earth, scorching it time and again until he was finally stopped by Thor, knocking him out of the sky with his mighty thunder bolt, sending him crashing into the sea.

The Haida Indians of the Queen Charlotte Islands have a legend that says that after the flood a raven or crow found a bunch of frightened little Indians hiding in a giant clam shell and had to coax them out. Being coaxed out by the raven, a totem of the Matriarch, suggests they were coaxed out into a Godless world, and the Indians of northern British Columbia and Yukon claim that in the beginning they and the wolf were brothers. This may have some bearing behind the movement protesting the controls of the wolf population in northern British Columbia and Yukon. The superstition dating back to the Matriarch in the beginning, "When men were maimed for confronting her and for killing her Holy Wolves."

These legends do contribute some evidence that there might have been more to the flood than just excessive rain. The Deucalian account starts with fire and ends with water and compares favorably with the theories expressed here. *The Dictionary of Classical Mythology* implies it was a combination of fire and water which still further substantiates the proposed theory.

The fact that it was at the end of the Iron Age and not at the beginning no doubt allows man enough time to develop weapons, maybe along similar lines to the ones we have today.

There is also the fact that Soloman said, "There is nothing new under the sun, what is going to be has been already." How this parallels this modern day Britain and America!

Scene XVI overlaps or is simultaneous to Scene XV.

SCENE XVI
ADAM THOR OR ANDVARI IS CAPSIZED FROM HIS SHIP BY LOKI OR SUTT (ABEL)

Cain has extracted the iron spike from the wound in Adam Thor's head and is nursing him back to health. While Adam is convalescing he takes a boat and goes fishing. Now I don't believe Adam is after fish, I think he is fishing for men. All the while Adam has been wounded there have been some who have spoken up for him, but they are only a few. Cain has been trying to recruit more.

While Adam Thor is convalescing on this fishing trip, Abel comes along as a pirate and sinks Adam's ship. Now this equates with the war and the sinking of the continents, namely Adam's Atlantis; or as recorded in the Bible, the flood.

1222

Fig. 22—Thor or Andvara being upset by Loki or Sutt. From Elamite seal, *c.* 3000 B.C. Note the Goat form of front paddler designating Thor by the Goat rebus of his name, and similarly the Lion-Wolf for Loki in the second following boat. The Sumer word-signs respectively read *Bur*, a common Eddic and Sumer title of Thor or In-Dara, and LUKH, *i.e.,* "Loki." (After *British Edda,* L.A. Waddell.)

We see in the Gawain romance the Fisher King (Adam Thor) on his sick bed, wounded, near death. His wounds being the cause for the kingdom being a void wasteland. The rebellion of his subjects being his wound, resulting in war and the destruction of the Earth. Gawain's quest for the Grail is the search for truth, knowledge and righteousness to restore the land to fertility.

This is demonstrated in the lament for Tammuz published by Mr. Langdon in Tammuz and Ishtar, and also in Sumerian and Babylonian Psalms.

"In Eanna, high and low, there is weeping,
Wailing for the house of the lord they raise.
The wailing is for the plants; the first lament is 'they grow not.'
The wailing is for the barley; the ears grow not.
For the habitations and flocks it is; they produce not.
For the perishing wedded ones, for perishing children it is; the dark-headed people create not.
The wailing is for the great river; it brings the flood no more.
The wailing is for the fields of men; the gunu grows no more.
The wailing is for the fish-ponds, the dasuhur fish spawn not.
The wailing is for the cane-brake; the fallen stalks grow not.
The wailing is for the forests; the tamarisks grow not.
The wailing is for the highlands; the masgam trees grow not.
The wailing is for the garden store-house; honey and wine are produced not.
The wailing is for the meadows; the bounty of the garden, the sihtu plants grow not.
The wailing is for the palace; life unto distant days is not."

This could very well describe a land devastated by nuclear war.

Adam Andavari Fishing from a Sailing-boat, Discovers Loki-Baldr as a Pirate

Loki (Sutt) quoths:
What is this fish, that runs with the flood,
And kens not to ware hisself with wit of danger?
Redeem thy head whole, by loosening your gold
To me the Finn of the glowing linden lance!

Andvari: Andvari I'm hight. Oinn is my father.
Many a force-stream have I fared,
Tho' a tender weird shaped my fate in olden days
That I shouldn't even wade in water.

L: Say thee Andvari, if thou wilt keep,
Thy life a little longer,
What gild-fee must men's sons pay
Who hack through their plighted word?

A: Over-great fee must men's sons pay,
They must wade the yelling wade:
Eating their words and lying to another
Leads to a long rod (flogging).

That (crime) shall gold e'en in gusts (ne'er pay)
'Tween brothers that ban their bargain,
And that slander Odl-ing's race,
But maun be my fee with thee that art no man's mate.

L: Gold is here for thee now, and now thou'st gotten gild
Mickle for mine head.
But thy son shall have no luck with it:
That reward shall bane ye both.

A: Thou gav'st the gift, but not a gift of love,
Thou gav'st it not with a hale heart.
Thy life should I have for forfeit,
If I witted thou wast brewing harm.

L: There's a worse fate in store for thee, I think.
Thy offspring's woe will bitter be:
Those yet unborn are under our curse,
And that while hatreds we all hug.

The weird's doom thou'lt have off the Ness
By the hand of thy 'friend' Apa (Abel).
In the water thou'lt be drown'd, if thou run with the
    wind
All is fey-death fixed aforehand.

L: Holed art thou George-the-Red! Hast thou yet
    drowned?
Mickle art thou humbled! Art thou going from me?
And from all my chosen people, and from Wodan's
    (sons?) favour?
Manifold time I told thee, and little thou minded
Me, thy wily 'friend'!
Thy mace I've laid low my friend,
All in the driving dripping waves!
Egg on Mōdi my chosen one! Now maun I have you
    Ygg.
Rough is the wrath of the Dis folk.
Now kennest thou Wodan ('s son) by sight!
Come nigh me if thou canst!

If we take a moment to compare some of the legends from around the world which spring from this event, we will find it quite revealing.

Firstly, we have Pro-Metheus Bound. Here we see Adam staked and chained to a rock in purgatory forever, insuring no savior will return to challenge Abel's rule of this world. If you notice it was not God who capsized Adam's ship, it was Abel-Sutt, or rather man influenced by Abel-Sutt (Satan). So we can conclude from the preceding that God did not destroy the world by the flood, it was Satan. God promises to stop Satan from destroying the world a second time.

R.S.V. Gen. 9:11 I establish my covenant with you, that never again shall all flesh be cut off by the waters of a flood, and never again shall there be a flood to destroy the earth.'' And God said, ''This is the sign of the covenant which I make between me and you and every living creature that is with you, for ALL future generations. I set my bow in the cloud, and it shall be a sign of the covenant between me and the earth.''

Fig. 23—Trial of "Adam, Son of God" (In-Dur or An-Dara) for breaking the arm of Šūti. (From Babylonian seal of about 2500 B.C.) (After *British Edda*, L.A. Waddell.)

It appears in figure 23 that Adam Thor was brought to trial before the Semitic God Anu, the God of this world (Abel) for breaking the arm of the South Wind (Abel). That was for a mere man (God personified as Adam Thor) casting down a divinity, the God of this world's rule of suppression and replacing it with the Rule of Reason, the light of truth and knowledge.

In the seal we see the Semitic God Anu seated, judging Adam Thor, who is accused by his own. His accusor has a Gothic horned headdress but feet of a crow holding a lizard in his hand being righteous in appearance only, with the restraining hand of a spirit of heaven on his arm.

This is somewhat a mock trial as there is only one God, he being God, was judged by God, he must have been judged by himself. In other words he took full responsibility of man's inability to handle the knowledge which he had taught them, as we see what actually happened step by step and then comparing.

Adam and his Goths came to this world to elevate man from the degenerate state to which he had fallen, suppressed by the Matriarch of Eden and her lover son Abel. Adam civilized them, educated them, gave them the moral code and befriended them. Man responded, appreciative of his better way of life. The more they advanced the more intensive became their education. Advancement in science increased to the Atomic Age. By this time Abel had been sending his spies to spy on them and had gained a lot of knowledge from them. Being Edenites they turned their newly learned knowledge into weapons. Adam, knowing this would happen, built weapons to deter them, to maintain peace, until man had acquired enough knowledge to become perfect. Abel had infiltrated into their midst and was spreading hate, greed, and fear, propagandizing among them. They lost faith in Adam and listened to themselves and they heard themselves say we have been tricked. Perfection is unobtainable, Adam was evil, he was leading them into destruction. It was his fault that man used his knowledge to make weapons of destruction. Coming to these conclusions they believed themselves more righteous, accusing their own God of evil, demanding he be tried by the God of this world, Abel. Adam was tried and found guilty of befriending and teaching man and sentenced to death, or as in Prometheus' case, staked and chained to a rock in purgatory forever, insuring no saviour for mankind. This compares to another mock trial, the trial of Jesus Christ.

Jesus was accused by the High Priests of the temple, considering themselves as God, or next to God on Earth. Jesus was accused of befriending and teaching man the good news of the Kingdom of Heaven by his own people. There was a restraining hand, portrayed as the Spirit of Heaven, on the arms of the persecuting Jewish High Priests, preventing them from stoning Jesus, as was their custom of putting criminals to death.

Jesus was taken and tried before the God of this world, which at that time was the Roman Empire which embraced Satan's religion of the Matriarch Mother Mary and her paramour son (Abel). Jesus was sentenced to death by crucifixion on their sacred pine tree of Eden. It was Pilate who pronounced him dead, an official of the Roman Empire, Abel's or Satan's Empire. It was only Satan who claimed Jesus dead. The true Church of Sunworship knew he was not dead.

It seems pertinent here to give a brief history of the Romish Church. It was founded in Hannibal's time. The Romans, in 204 B.C., were weary from their long struggle with Hannibal and to cheer their drooping spirits they adopted an Oriental Goddess which prophecy had revealed would drive the foreign invaders from their soil. Ambassadors were sent to her sacred city of Pessinus in Phrygia. "The small black stone which embodied the mighty divinity was entrusted to them and conveyed to Rome, where it was received with great respect and installed in the Temple of Victory on the Palatine Hill. We may conjecture, though we are not told, that the Mother of the Gods brought with her the worship of her youthful lover or son to her new home in the West. Certainly the Romans were familiar with the Galli, the emasculated priest of Attis, before the close of the Republic. These unsexed beings, in their oriental costume, with little images suspended on their breasts, appear to have been familiar sights in the streets of Rome." Page 404, *Golden Bough*.

Those of the Roman Catholic faith, please don't take offense. Your church is but a wayward bride; nurtured with tender loving care, she will return to her husband, her true lover, and the light of truth will lighten the whole world like the Sun one day in the future.

Now, we compare the legends of Adonis and Attis, we will first try to understand the myth. The name Adonis is a corruption of Adon: "Lord," a title of honour transformed into a proper name by the Greeks. Adonis is supposedly the tree spirit and also the corn spirit and has been honoured by many rituals pertaining to the growing of crops and procuring sufficient water for the coming crop year. We must remember that these myths have been perpetuated by people unable to comprehend the actual event which they are perpetuating. They associate the facts with something tangible that they can understand. Their corn and other vegetables, trees and the life giving water to make them grow, result in a God of Nature, the birth of the God being immediately after the winter solstice and then somehow his death being the harvest of the corn and his resurrection being the new seed for the next year's cycle. This, in my opinion, is applying the same logic as my example of the birth of a legend.

Now, in actual fact, we can see what actually happened and who Adonis actually is. We will compare Adonis' death with the plight of Pro-Metheus.

Prometheus is on a ledge, high up in the mountains of Scythia, lying chained and spiked to a rock in eternal torment. His wife Asia, bitterly lamenting his plight, sits by his side. His son, by whom he was released, sits beneath him. His crime was befriending man and stealing fire from Heaven, sentenced by the God of this world.

Adonis is seen, his mangled body buried high on a ledge on Mt. Lebanon, a lonely, desolate spot, with his wife Aphrodite lamenting over his grave. He was killed by a wild boar or by the jealous Ares. Who is Ares? We have a clue in figure 24.

King Pisha's Rhinoceros seal as Priest King at Eden. The Rhinoceros on this seal as the name for Eden is interesting. That animal is called in Sumerian Pish which is homophonous with this Priest King's name of Pisha in both of his latter seals, but which is written by a different pictograph from that of the Rhinoceros. The latter pictograph was thus presumably used on this seal for word play. The Rhinoceros name in Chaldean or Semitic also means "Edin." The Sumerian word Pish for Rhinoceros with the pictogram shown in Fig. 24 is also defined as Wild Pig. So it looks

King PISHA'S Rhinoceros Seal as Priest-king at Edin

His seal with the Rhinoceros as its chief emblem is seen in Figure 24. Its inscription reads as follows:—

Seal.

Sumer (Mesop.).

Reads : PISH-A GUT-U ASH-MAR SIB-A EDIN-MA[2]

Transl.: PISHA the *Gutu*, the One (or Eldest) son, the Shepherd at *Edin* (or Rhinoceros) Land.

Fig. 24—Seal of PISHA the *Gutu* at *Edin* Land deciphered. [1]Related Pig sign here clearly figured as a horned Rhinoceros. [2]This sign seems to be a conventionalized ship-sign *ma* which, as we have seen, means also "land," for *Ma* is the shortened form of *Mad,* "land." (Afer *Makers of Civilization,* L.A. Waddell.)

as if Ares is an Edenite. As we saw earlier Loki or Abel was also wooing Eve and we see Adam as the gardener Goth introducing agriculture to this world, thus accounting for his title of corn spirit. The myth goes on to say when Adonis was wounded by the Wild Pig white roses sprung from his blood. Aphrodite, hastening to her wounded lover, trod on a bush of white roses, the thorns tearing her feet, and her sacred blood dyed the roses red forever more. Thus, if I am not mistaken, we have the emblem of the Rosecrucian's, the rose and the cross.

The red rose, to this day, is the symbol of love and the partly opened rose, is man's becoming aware of his God.

The ritual of Adonis, the date of which is not definitely known but probably in the spring, was to celebrate in effigy the dead Adonis, mourn over him, then carry him to the ocean and throw him into the water. The next day they would rejoice saying Adonis has risen. Now, if we compare Adonis with Adam Thor we see a striking resemblance. Adam Thor was wounded by Abel-Sutt and then later capsized in his boat and dunked in the ocean. Abel, thinking him drowned was surprised when he swam to shore and avenged himself by breaking his arm. The Edenites on the beach, watching Adam's fight with Abel and lending him their sword is symbolic of mankind realizing that Adam was right and Abel was responsible for the destruction. The people came back to him and his religion and he was their God again. This also equals Aphrodites running to her wounded lover. Women are symbolic of the Church; when Adonis (Adam) was wounded the Church returned to him. Of course, the Church is the congregation.

These same ceremonies are celebrated in India. In both of them, the marriage of two divine beings, whose affinity with vegetation seems to be identical and whose effigy was mourned over and later thrown into the sea. This apparently gives a common ancestry to these myths from India, Syria, Greece, Egypt and Britain.

We will find that the myth of Attis is the most interesting. We find that he was killed by a wild boar, also. That tells us he was killed by the Edenites, the same as Adonis, and he was killed by his own hands also; castrating himself, he bled to death under the sacred pine tree of Eden and from his blood violets grew, as compared with roses and anemones from Adonis' blood.

This also signifies the mock trial of Adam Thor being God and being judged by and sentenced by God, there only being one God he must have judged and condemned himself; and also the perversion by Satan and the reasoning of man. If promiscuity and prostitution in Adam's higher civilization was sin then they reasoned all sex was sin. To attain perfection one must be sinless, to be sinless one must abstain from sin, sex included, which leads to the extinction of the race, therefore perfection is unobtainable. As we saw with Adam Thor and his civilization the more knowledge you acquire the more perfect you have to become to handle it. That is the point Abel-Seth was putting across to man, perfection is unobtainable. Appeal to the lusts of your basic nature and the Goddess of Fertility, so worship the Mother Goddess and indulge in promiscuity until your lusts are content. The more children born the more enslaved to them you become, eventually taxing the land to its limits, living on the edge of starvation, keeping them in poverty preoccupied with scratching an existence out of the ground with their primitive tools, allowing no time for education and advancement in knowledge. By worshipping the Goddess of Fertility, they were perpetuating the vicious cycle, enslaving themselves to the consequences. By this means the Matriarch El, the Mother Goddess of the serpent cult of Eden, keeps man in suppression. We will come back to the perversion of the rituals in a later scene. Attis is portrayed as being hung with his arms above his head on the sacred pine of Eden and pierced in the side with a spear.

Quoted from a verse of the *Havamal*—

"I know that I hung on the windy tree
    For nine whole nights,
    Wounded with a spear, dedicated to Odin
    Myself to myself"

According to ancient Christian tradition, Christ was crucified on the 25th of March regardless of the phase of the moon. The death and resurrection of Attis was officially celebrated in Rome on the 24th to the 27th of March, also.

Attis was also a God of nature and plants and also the tree spirit, the same as Adonis and Osiris; the tree being Adam's sacred tree, the Rowan-ash, the tree of life.

As legend has it Adonis and Attis were born from Myrah trees, the bark bursting after ten months pregnancy. A boar rooting at the tree with its tusk opened it up, allowing the birth of the babe. This probably is based on the assumption that the more Abel tried to destroy the tree of life, the more life issued from it.

The myth of Osiris of Egypt is basically the same theme as Adonis. Osiris was born on the 25th of December, he was a God of vegetation introducing agriculture to Egypt and later, leaving Egypt in care of his wife Isis, went around the world teaching agriculture. He is accredited with the introduction of cereal grains. He was tricked by Zyphen (Abel or Satan) to get into a coffin which he immediately sealed and threw in the river and drowned. He was found by Isis, who was lovelorn, hunting up and down the river for him. His body was then torn into fourteen pieces by a wild boar of which we understand is the picture-graph for Eden, so therefore Abel or Satan, and scattered all over Egypt, later resurrected to become the God of the dead. He was also for awhile sealed inside a tree.

The Myth of Dionysus

Again we see a God of agriculture and the tree spirit honoured as the patron of all fruit trees, especially the apple and fig.

He was also, the God of the Vine and the maker of wine, he also died a violent death and was resurrected again. He is even identified by name, Bakus the Second King, the son of Adam Thor Cain. As true to history he himself is spoken of as doing the work of a husbandman, he is reported to have been the first to yoke oxen to the plough. The rest of this myth is so perverted that little can be gleaned. If we look at how violently they died we should realize there must have been a reason for such violence to have been recorded, we will run through each in turn. Adonis—his bones were ground in a mill and scattered to the wind. Quote from Burn's *John Barleycorn:* "They wasted o'er a scorching flame, but the miller used him worst of all. The marrow of his bones, for he crushed him between two stones."

Attes was severed in two while hanging on the tree allowing the lower half to wallow in the gore at the foot of the tree.

Osiris and Dionysus were hacked into fourteen pieces and scattered all over Egypt.

Why would different nations of different tongues all celebrate in their mythology an event which happened in the same time period, approximately 3360 B.C. which corresponds to the time period of the flood as recorded not only in the Old Testament but in every legend and myth around the whole world? Why have their hero destroyed so violently and completely and them have him resurrected which is an absolute impossibility? All cling to this myth. Why if it did not originate from one single event? All accept one legendary history that beams a ray of light into the dark mythological period illuminating the fragments of truth. More will be said on this when we deal with the perversions of these myths. We will run through them seeing what they all have in common.

They each worshipped him as the benefactor of humanity, he is the spirit of the tree, no doubt the tree of life and also the fruit trees and the grape vine. He is worshipped as the God of Agriculture, grain and corn by all. They all have him completely destroyed, severed in half, torn into pieces and scattered all over the country or ground up and blown to the wind. In the case of Attis he went willingly to his death. As he is made to say, "Dedicated to Odin, Myself to Myself." He stepped willingly into the coffin as Osiris and was drowned. As Adonis his body is thrown into the sea as compared with Adam Thor being dunked in the ocean with the fish. As Attis he is nailed to a pine tree and pierced in the side with a spear on the 25th of March, comparing identically to Jesus, the second Adam. Odin of the Edda, myself to myself. As Dionysus he is named Bakus (Cain) the Son of Adam and was the first to yoke oxen to the plough. Finally we saw all were killed or mutilated by a wild boar which we saw is the pictograph for Eden. Therefore, they were killed by Abel of the wolf-serpent worshipping cult of the Matriarch of Eden. Out of their blood grew something beautiful, in all legends.

All these perverted mythological Gods can without a doubt be traced back to the one original Adam Thor of the British Edda.

Now, we will see what Adam Thor has to say about all this. Adam Thor admits that Abel-Seth wounded him severely in the head and he lost a lot of blood and was on his sick bed for quite a while. Cain is tending his wounds, nursing him back to health. In the meanwhile Abel-Seth is proclaiming to the world that Adam Thor is dead. "I killed him—I am victorious!" To make good and sure, Abel-Seth declares war on Atlantis, resulting in complete destruction and the sinking of the continent. Not only does Abel-Seth say that Adam Thor is dead, but blown to pieces, drowned, ground up and blown to the wind, so completely destroyed that he will never gain face again. Adam Thor is accused of being the cause of the holocaust by educating man and teaching him the secrets of science and the secrets of the Gods. Never again, Satan thought, would man listen to God.

Thor now appears to have swam like a fish.

Fig. 25—Adam-Thor or Andvari as An-Dara, "Fish-Man of the Waters." From Assyrio-Babylonian stele. (After *British Edda*, L.A. Waddell.)

Adam's Revenge

L: Swain! O swain! where wert thou born?
                  What man's son art thou?
                  Thou has on Fafni redden'd thy flashing mace.
                  Stunn'd am I to the heart by thy hurter.

A: Sig, the Outlawed (of thy folk)—Sigurd—I'm
      called . . .
      Who has with thee waged weapons.

L: Rede I thee now Sig-the-Red, and take my rede
      And ride thee home hence! Leave thou
      My titbits of yellow gold and hoard o' red
       bangles o' fee-fine,
      Their worth will be thy bane (if taken).

A: Reding is for me rede. And ride I maun
      To that gold that's on the ling lying.
      And thou Fafni lie there, broken with fear,
      Lie there till Hell again have thee.

L to himself: Reg of the Inn has redden'd me. He maun rede
      me too!
      He maun be worth us both, his banes (Abel and
       Wodan).
      Fear sits on me. Lost, I think, art thou Faf mine!

L to Adam: Thy (Thor-Adam's) warrant now is the more
      mighty.

Adam Thor is Congratulated by an Edenite on His Victory over Sutt (Seth) the Wolf-Chief Oppressor

Edenite: Hail thee now Sig-the-Red! Now thou'rt victor in
      the fight,
      And Faf thou'st made to fear!
      Of men who tread the mould,
      Thou art, quoth I, the bravest of them all.

A: That can't be witted, till all come together,
      Of Sig's divine sons,
      Which is bravest of them all.
      There's many a worthy one who has never needed
      Redden his hurter in another's breast.

E: Glad art thou now Sig-the-Red, and fain glad in
      going,
      That thou thrust the Gram-wolf in the grass.

My brother has thou baned,
Tho' I myself had some share in't.

A: Thou jogg'd afar, meanwhile I Fafni redden'd
By my whetted hurter.
Afar from me, when I the mighty Orm (Dragon)
    matched,
Thou wast meantime biding in the heath.

E: Long might thou have lain in the heath (fighting)
With that old Edenite,
If thou had'st not the sword, I geared myself,
That whetted hurter of mine.

A: Courage is better than the mightiest blade,
When wrathful men shall fight.
I've seen the man in a hasty fight.
With a slab for a sword win the fray:
The brave fares better than the craven
In the ashen game of war:
The gladsome man fares better than the bawler
With whatever comes to his hand.

The sinking of Adam Thor's boat, or continent by Abel-Seth made Adam Thor angry. He swore he would break Abel's arm for this. He is quite a way out in the ocean, but he starts swimming. Apparently it takes him three days to swim to shore. On reaching shore he proceeds to take his revenge on Abel-Seth, battling with him and breaking his arm as he said he would do, putting Abel out of commission for awhile. The survivors realized they had been beguiled by Abel-Seth and it wasn't Adam Thor that was to blame, it was Abel-Seth and his evil ways that was to blame for the disaster. On seeing Adam Thor they rejoiced and he became their God again and they became his people. What else could they say after listening to Abel-Seth who had told them for so long that he was dead? Anything other than he is "resurrected".

Our present era, the post-flood world is paralleling the Antidiluvian period with a remarkable degree of repetition: making the prophecies of the scriptures written by the men who were entrusted with the secrets of the Holy Grail or sometimes called the Mountain Stone, less mystifying and more readily understood.

The parallel which we can draw today should be a lesson to us. The Caldee Semitic, or Edenites as I refer to them, are accusing the Aryan race for being the light of the world, the educators, the uplifters of man, of teaching them the mysteries of the Cosmos and the laws of science. The Edenites being immature, harboring evil in their minds; that is greed, hate, envy, jealousy and so forth; are tools in the hands of Abel, who is manipulating them to further his purpose with the same game plan as he used the first time. They couldn't resist the temptation to turn their new found knowledge into weapons of destruction. Abel, manipulating the Edenites, infiltrated into the Aryan kingdom. Sowing the seeds of greed, selfishness, hate, and envy. Falling on fertile ground, these seeds sprouted and grew like weeds, choking out patriotism, morality, pride and integrity and blooming into lust, hate, greed and sensual pleasures as it is obvious to see by the enmity between management and labour. We have the highest standard of living in the world and we still want more, for less! Pornography, the worship of sex, is running rampant, people with no direction are blowing their minds on drugs.

Our Aryan leaders see the menacing threat of the Edenites. Through befriending, educating and financing them they can bring peace to this planet. In the meantime we have to maintain a strong arm to deter aggression and maintain peace by power which is our God given responsibility as we will see later.

Arming themselves thus, people came to realize that with their carnal nature, thinking and living like Edenties but desiring to live in peace like Aryans, they would be unable to control their actions. They saw that their destruction and annihilation would be inevitable, just a matter of time. Divided among themselves, in their confusion not knowing the direction, each going their own way. With their limited vision they saw their folly. Crediting themselves with the wisdom of seeing this folly, they thought themselves wise. They accused their government and Aryan leaders of being evil for acquiring knowledge, and unraveling the mysteries of science, and demand they be judged by world opinion.

In our vanity we deem ourselves to be wise, yet all our Churches are at variance with each other, groping in the half light; and politicians are hungry for power. If we allow ourselves to be led, instead of leading, we will end up in the jaws of the trap set by Abel-Sutt.

You only have to turn on the television and listen to the news and you will hear small third world nations, jealous and envious of the Western Powers; the powers whose sin is befriending, feeding, educating and financing them, developing their resources, buying it from them, converting their resources into money so they can afford to educate their people and develop their country; pointing an accusing finger, and accusing us of being a threat to their very existence and of this world with our peace keeping arsenal of nuclear weapons. European nations are condemning us for deploying missles on their soil. Our churches are condemning us for maintaining peace by power. Even our own citizens are rising in protest against money allocated in the budget for the defense and safety of all nations. If the great Aryan leaders of this era are ignored and replaced by self-righteous do-gooders with no understanding of the plan and purposes of life and disarmament of the West begins then the prophecy of God, or rather the promises of Satan, will surely come about.

"There is a purpose being worked out here below," as quoted by Sir Winston Churchill. The nuclear age is with us, we can't make the knowledge we know go away.

It is only another stage in our development. It is like when we were in school passing up into grade eleven; we found it more difficult to cope with; the lessons became harder; there was no reason, if we took the time to understand the nature of the lessons and worked diligently, that we wouldn't eventually graduate.

There seem to be three steps in the process of obtaining perfection. After all, that is what we are qualifying for.

Firstly, man must learn to control his actions. The lower levels, or the less civilized or educated man, when confronted with a dispute quickly turns to force resulting in fighting and killing. Prov. 15:18: "A hot tempered man stirs up strife, but he who is slow to anger quiets contention."

Secondly, man must learn to control his tongue. Psalm 34:13: "Keep your tongue from evil, and your lips from speaking deceit. By controlling the tongue man can avoid confrontations of force."

Finally, man must learn to control his thoughts. Matthew 15:19: "From out of the heart comes evil thoughts, murder, adultery, fornification, theft, false witness, slander." If man can control his thoughts his tongue would be controlled, consequently his actions would also be under control.

We have many great minds forging ahead, acquiring knowledge, educating and uplifting the multitudes, advancing them according to the master plan. Man is slow to accept new ideas. He rebels against change and advancement but he is caught up and swept along in the tide of this era of enlightenment whether he likes it or not, whether it be religion or science.

We are living in the nuclear age now, in fact we have always been living in the nuclear age. Our creators know all the secrets, they could destroy us any time at will but we trust their righteous thoughts, we have faith in them; therefore, we don't fear them. We even put our trust in them to save us in the time of our great tribulation; an atomic holocaust as we interpret it today.

Matthew 24:21 "For then there will be great tribulation, such as has not been from the beginning of the world until now, no and never will be." And if those days had not been shortened, no human beings would be saved (alive).

We have faith in Christ that he will stop this holocaust by use of powers so great that it will pale our weapons into insignificance.

Matthew 24:29 "Immediately after the tribulation of those days the sun will be darkened, and the moon will not give its light and the stars will fall from the heaven, and the powers of the heaven will be shaken; then will appear the sign of the son of man in heaven, and then all the tribes of the earth will mourn, and they will see the son of man coming on the clouds of heaven with power and great glory."

If our God has knowledge of powers so great he can shake the very heavens and we trust that power to save us from annihilating ourselves. Why can't we trust those who were delegated the responsibility by Adam Thor of maintaining peace on this earth? Once we find out who they are, give them our individual support, and insist they live up to their responsibility.

Self-preservation is motive enough for man to explore all avenues open to him to insure his survival, arms and defense are no exception. Development of increasingly more sophisticated weapons only guarantees our defense and the safety of the world, over which we must not relinquish our lead for if we do, we will be at the mercy of irrational men.

With this research will come new inventions. Eventually the day will come, although it will be fought against tooth and nail, it will be decried, damned and condemned and especially by those who wish to keep their right to sin; but the time will come when electronic devices will be devised that can intercept a man's thoughts. Then the very nature of his heart will be laid bare, when this happens man will be forced to control his thoughts. When he has mastered the control of his thoughts he will be perfect as is his creator.

Don't think this is impossible, we already have the lie detector. Science fiction has already accepted it. The movie Brain Storm is a good example, and we have truth serums. Science fiction is our fairy tale for the future. Ideas thought of by great minds, keeping one step ahead, preparing the minds of men and women to accept the new truths of the future as they come.

The final step in the order of things on this Earth is control of ones own thoughts. This will be Abel-Seth's last stand. It will be fought with all fury. The invasion of the privacy of ones thoughts will be condemned, but it will get used to controlling our thoughts, just as we got used to controlling our actions for fear of the consequence. Like we control our tongue in public for fear of being embarrassed by our thoughts. We will learn to accept the fact that we have to control our thoughts in public so we don't expose our devious nature and embarrass ourselves.

Abel-Seth is already defending his position against the time when we will be able to comprehend the inner thoughts of men. Not word for word, but to be able to perceive whether a man's thoughts are honorable or devious by the brightness or color of his aura. It can be better explained by the story of Pinnochio when his nose grew longer each time he told a lie. The moral here would be to never buy a car from a used car salesman with a nose over six inches long.

Luke 9:46—"And an argument arose among them as to which of them was the greatest. But when Jesus perceived the thoughts of their hearts he took a child and put him by his side, and said to them 'Whoever receives this child in my name is receiving me.'"

It was normal for Jesus to perceive a man's thoughts. This is how Jesus will rule with a rod of iron. He will be able to read men's thoughts, therefore he will be able to judge fairly. Abel-Seth, however is already removing shame from the minds of men and cloaking it in a disguise of honesty. How can a man's evil thoughts shame him if he has no shame?

Members of this society, rock singers and such, are making themselves look as degenerate as possible. Others proclaim to the world that they are perverts and deviates; even ministers of the churches are professing to be homosexuals. In other words, man is starting to proclaim new freedoms, a freedom from guilt. Expose your sins and evil nature and be proud of it in the guise of being honest with yourself.

In the days when Adam Thor and his Aryans ruled his Rule of Reason had been rejected and man had lost his direction. Man took the destiny of the world on himself. In his confusion, he could see war and their destruction was inevitable.

They set about making monuments to their civilization, these structures were virtually indestructible. They located them in areas of the world which would be outside the area of the hottest conflict. These monuments contained the sum total of all knowledge accumulated to that date. They were built for posterity, if any life survived the pending war they would have the accumulation of knowledge preserved to rebuild their world. The same thought applies today; we have time capsules so that in the event of a nuclear war, or if all life is annihilated at some future time, if an intelligent race visited this planet they would find a record of our accomplishments. These great monuments, the time capsules of the past, are the great pyramids of Egypt and South America.

The pyramid of most interest, the one that has confounded man the most, is the Great Pyramid of Cheops. You may say this pyramid is a time capsule containing all the known knowledge of the past civilization and it was intended to enlighten posterity; any life which survived the disaster could have access to their wealth of knowledge and continue on from where they left off. If that being the case, you may say it has failed miserably. In the stead of enlightening man it has confounded him in a shroud of mystery. The mere fact that it has mystified man instead of enlightening him all these ages only strengthens my theory and leads me to believe that it was in fact designed and built for that purpose. That, odd as it may seem, will be dealt with in a future chapter.

There have been many theories brought forth over the ages on the purpose of these great structures, from tombs to temples to surveying theodolites to beacons for interterrestrial space travelers. The mystery of the Great Pyramid of Cheops had been probed for two thousand years by scientists without revealing its secrets. The design of the pyramid makes it virtually indestructible. The outward appearance is such that all sides slope into the center making it impossible for them to fall outward, and the inside is ninety-nine percent solid making it impossible for them to collapse inwardly. The Rosecrucian order and the Free Masons have suggested there are at least three more chambers and secret passageways yet undiscovered and a passageway somewhere beneath the northwest corner of the pyramid which leads to the sphinx. Even so they are still dense enough that inward collapse would be impossible as is evident in the fact that the seventy ton granite monaliths which support the ceiling of the kings chamber are cracked and the pyramid still stands as it has for thousands of years, proving they were suitably constructed for the purpose for which they were designed. They withstood the destructive forces unleashed at the time when the ancient civilization was destroyed. (The discovery of some red paint cartouches dubbed on the inner walls of the upper chambers of the kings chamber were thought to belong to Khufu, believed to be the second Pharaoh of the fourth Dynasty, called Cheops by the Greeks. Doubt still lingers that there might have been a far earlier king with a similar cartouche which only emphasizes my theory. Page 65, *Secrets of the Great Pyramid*).

There is no record in Egyptian history of the construction or purpose of the Great Pyramid. Anything of such colossus and precision could only have been built by a race with a highly advanced knowledge of mathematics and capabilities of such grandeur that its construction would not have made its mark and be recorded in the annals of their history, unless of course it was ancient to the Pharaoh's of Egypt and was a mystery to them, too.

The writings of Herodotus in his *History of Egypt,* which was written about 440 B.C., fail to reveal the builders or the purpose of the Pyramid.

If the Pyramid was just the tomb of an ancient Egyptian Pharaoh why did the founding fathers of America place an unfinished pyramid on the dollar bill? Why was the constitutional convention; on May 25th, 1787 in Philadelphia; of twelve states represented by the most remarkable body of men ever to assemble anywhere? Why does one of the Obelisks erected in Egypt by Thutmose III now stand in Central Park, as it was intended when it was erected many centuries ago to stand in the country where the eagle spreads its wings? Why is the eagle the national emblem of the U.S.A.? Why did Jesus say (Matthew 24:28), "Wherever the body is, there the eagles will be gathered."

In the early Christian period there was a great move afoot to suppress knowledge and to stamp out any evidence of the true Aryan, or Gothic, Solar-religion and replace it with their version of Catholic Christianity. We are all well aware of the legend of Romulus and Remus, the wolf suckled founders of Rome in Italy; identifying them with the Wolf tribe of the Mother Son cult of the Roms. ("Moreover, Rom or Romit was the title of the set-Wolf and Serpent worshipping aborigine's of ancient Egypt, and "Romany" is the title of the dark, non-Aryan, fortune telling gypsies and weirds of Roumania and elsewhere of the Mediterranean or Iberian race; and the present day Moslem title of "Rum" for Asia Minor and their religious capital at Constantinople was not borrowed from the Italian "Rome" as is generally supposed." Page 277, *British Edda.*)

This attempt was made by the Roman Emporer Theodosius in 389 A.D. when under his orders a Catholic Christian mob sacked the library at Alexandria. Furthermore, he is accredited with being beneficial to the Christian Church. He virtually eliminated Aryanism and paganism throughout his empire. The plunge into the Dark Ages and suppression had begun. If there had been any record of the purpose of the pyramids it was surely lost with the destruction of knowledge contained in those libraries.

It is interesting to note that the passageways are very small, only fifty inches or two cubits square. They would have been very difficult to make by men of normal height. Obviously it wasn't a lack of space that made them so small; is it possible then that they were made by small people? As we learned from the Edda the aboriginal people were very small. It also leads one to wonder if the pygmy tribes of Africa couldn't be of the original creation, lost in the jungles of Africa, keeping to themselves and not having the effect of the Aryan or Edenite upbreeding.

The belief that the Great Pyramid was a tomb is an extravagance that would far exceed the vanity of any Pharaoh and there was no mummy found in it, either. The passageways were all sealed and plugged with limestone and granite blocks, sealing the Great Pyramid. What appears to be a sarcophagus, the tomb of the Pharaoh Cheops, is nothing but an empty coffer, oddly enough the same dimensions as the arc of the covenant. Maybe it was the original of their standard of measure preserved for posterity.

The measurements of the Great Pyramid have been of great interest to all the scientists who have challenged its mystery and probed the secrets which have confounded man for so many centuries. It seems that all who have tried to fathom the purpose of the pyramids existence seem to have a germ of an idea in the back of their heads which keeps nagging at them that at least part of the secret lies in the measurements.

Sir Isaac Newton; 1642–1727, an English natural philosopher, mathematician and master of the brotherhood; in order to prove his theory of gravitation needed an accurate measurement of the Earth. For this he needed a standard unit of measure which he found in the sacred Cubit of the Jews, which was twenty five English inches.

Later John Taylor was to take up the riddle of the Great Pyramid. Taking the measurements of Howard Vyse (page 70, *Secrets of The Great Pyramids*) Taylor then discovered that if he divided the perimeter of the pyramid by twice its height it gave him a quotient of 3.144, remarkably close to the value of pi which is computed as 3.14159.

Taylor came to the conclusion that if the incommensurable value of pi was incorporated into the design of the pyramid it must have been built by someone with advanced mathematical knowledge as it was not until sixth century A.D. that a Hindu, possibly of the Aryan race, Arya-Bhata worked pi out to the fourth decimal.

(Page 71, *Great Pyramid*) The oldest known document which indicates that Egyptians had a knowledge of the value of pi is the Rhind Papyrus, dated about 1700 B.C. and therefore much later than the Pyramid. It was found in the wrappings of a mummy in 1855 by Henry Alexander Rhind, it is now in the British Museum. It gives a rough value for pi of 3.16. This fact suggests that although pi was incorporated in the pyramids it was unknown prior to 1700 B.C. Having only a rough value for pi and keeping it in such a place of honor as in the wrappings of a mummy it seems likely it was newly acquired knowledge which they were very proud of. Pondering the Pyramid could have been a preoccupation of the Egyptians in those days, too.

(Page 2, *Great Pyramid*) No description of the pyramid has survived in Egyptian text. Legends have it painted in various colors, marked with designs and inscribed with symbols. The thirteenth century Arab historian, Abd-al-Latif, says the Pyramid was once inscribed with unintelligible characters in inscriptions so numerous they would fill ten thousand pages.

The casing stones were stripped from the Pyramid around the fourteenth century to rebuild the earthquake shattered cities, losing forever the hope of deciphering the message contained in the inscriptions. Another amazing fact of the Pyramid is that its builders not only incorporated the pi properties but also the constant proportion Phi and is known as the golden section or 1.618.

With the incorporation of pi and Phi in the Pyramid the spherical quarters of the Northern Hemisphere could be converted to flat areas. Thus the Northern Hemisphere is represented in the Great Pyramid and accurate measurements of the world can be determined from it.

Another interesting fact is that dead animals don't seem to putrify, they just dehydrate. That would make the pyramids an excellent store house for anything to be kept for eons of time. Substantiating the legend that Enoch, foreseeing the deluge to come by the signs in the stars, built the Pyramid to preserve books of science and knowledge and other worthwhile artifacts from destruction and ruin.

There are other interesting facts which I will briefly mention. The use of electronic sounding devices for the detection of secret chambers and passageways were to no avail as the information became garbled. Used, dull razor blades, when placed in the Pyramid, regained their sharp cutting edge again. They also seem to be condensers or generators of electricity. All these facts and many more are delved into in great detail in Peter Tompkins' book, *Secrets of the Great Pyramid*. I suggest anyone wishing to substantiate the facts which I have glossed over regarding the Pyramid should read Peter Tompkins' book.

I strongly believe that the builders of the pyramids; being so far advanced in astronomy, mathematics, geometry, science, the knowledge of creation, and the cosmos; would not have lost their civilization, both in Egypt and South America, at apparently the same time without being the result of a traumatic disaster.

The decline of ancient knowledge may be attributed to such men as Alexander the Great and Theodosus. With the sacking of Persephalis and the dismantling and moving of the great university of Heliopolis to his capital of Alexandria where the Alexandria geographers and philosophers, not fully understanding the advanced sciences contained in the volumes of the old library of Heliopolis, mishandled the misunderstood knowledge resulting in the beginning of the decline. The decline was completed by Theodosius with the sacking of Alexandria. If we attribute the loss and destruction of the knowledge of the old Egyptian pagan Solar-cult of Adam Thor to them, to whom do we attribute the loss and destruction of the ancient knowledge of the Sun-cult in South America? Could it be to Cortez and the Roman Catholic missionaries of the Mother and Lover Son-cult determined to stamp out all evidence of the original Solar-cult from the face of the earth?

If we suppose for a moment that this great ancient civilization of Egypt had its beginnings about 2700 B.C. springing forth from primitive man how do you account for another such phenomenon paralleling it some thousand miles across the Atlantic Ocean? Did these people; so far advanced in astronomy, mathematics, geometry and science; after building the pyramids in Egypt drift aimlessly on rafts of reed on the Atlantic Ocean until washing up on the shores of South America and hopping out built pyramids of a slightly different style, possibly older, and monuments to their Sun-God Ra, as some people have proposed?

Sufficient facts on the pyramids have been stated to establish the fact to the reader that there is vastly more to the pyramid than a colossal pile of masonry. The fact has also been established that after probing the mystery of the Great Pyramid of Cheops for two thousand years nobody really knows for sure who built them, when or why.

Part Two

SCENE XVII
ADAM THOR VISITS EDEN

Adam Thor or Cain has now established his second dynasty in Asia Minor at Enoch City. It is possible that this scene could be out of sequence as there is no mention of Cain. It may have been a visit by Adam Thor before the destruction of Atlantis. Either way it really doesn't matter. It's like riding the inner-circle subway, no matter where you get on you eventually get back from where you started. It just goes around and around.

Adam Thor Visits Eden

Chatting were the Asas all in the Thing
And the Asas ladies all in talk
About the rakish ruler Tiva (Baldr) saying:
Why have we baleful dreams about Baldr?

Up rose Od-O-the-Inn, the Gard'ner Goth
And on Slippy the saddle laid he,
Rode he aneath thence til Nif Hell.
Met he a whelp as he came to Or Hell:

It was bloody on its breast as (it ran on) afore
To the Gald (Chaldee) Father's, and it yelp'd for long.
Forward rode Od-O-the-Inn, a manifold way down
Till he came to the head of (El) Rann's Hell.

Then rode Od-inn to afore the East door,
As there wot he Vol Sibyl was lying,
Learned in the lore of the witchcraft of Val Gald,
He says (to himself): "Till need rise nae word will I
     quoth."

Adam Thor visits El the Old serpent Sibyl of Eden to try to
understand her thinking since Abel is raising some consternation
among the Asas and their ladies.

Adam is not going to Eden to prove a point or defend himself,
he doesn't have to. As he said, "Till need arises, I will say nothing." He just wants to find out who they think he is and what they
intend to do.

We must remember that he is asking the Matriarch El, so we
can't expect to get the whole truth. What we will get is the truth
with a perverted twist.

Adam's Interview with El, the Mother Serpent Sibyl of Eden

El quoths:	What's the man that's to me unknown
	That has waked me so tiresome soon?
	I was (dreaming) I was snow'd in snow and slush'd in rain
	And drenched with dew, and dead for long.
Thor:	Way-Tamer I'm hight, son am I of Wealth.
	Say thee me tidings of Hell and I'll tell of the Homes (Dale)!
	For whom are these benches with byrnies strewn,
	And the flat fairly flooded with shields?

E: Here stands for Baldr brew'd the mead,
But (Bil) the Baptist's beer lies shielded afar
In the mighty Asa (home) I ween.
Need I have said so? Now maun I tush!

T: Tush not thou Sibyl! Still will I pry
Until I know all, on will I wit:
Who is the man that's become Baldr's bane
And who Wodan's son in time will ruin?

E: Hoedr (Adam) bearing the Red (Rowan) barred
           twig (cross).
He maun become Baldr's bane,
And he Wodan's son in time will ruin.
Need I have said so? Now maun I tush! . . .
No common Way-Tamer art thou as I thought,
But thou'rt Od(-am)-o'-the-Inn, the Gard'ner Goth!

T: No (common) Sibyl art thou, nor (common) wise
           quean,
But thou art The Three Fates' mother!

(A simpler version of this visit to Eldi, as given in
the Sibyl's Lay, records that Adam on arriving
there is taunted by her with the desire of carrying
off her Magic oracular Stone Bowl or "Holy
Grail" of Eden, which he eventually did capture
as a war trophy.):

Alone sat she (El) outside, then in the Gard'ner
came, Young Yggi the Asa, and he looked her in
the eyes. "Who'd frighten me?" (quoth she).
"Why deceive me?

I know all Od(-am)-o'-the-Inn! I know where thine
eye has fallen.
'Tis on Mary's Mimi-well (the Magic Bowl),
Whence drink I the Mimi mead every morn!
Off as pledge (thou want'st it), Valiant Father!"

She tells him he is Adam Thor of the Rowan Cross, that he
has been a bane to her son Abel-Sutt and that in time Abel-Sutt

will be victorious over Adam Thor's Rule of Reason, that he will rule the world.

As I said before, Abel-Sutt has had a hand in editing and bending the scriptures, so we must be very careful when reading them so that we can differentiate between the prophecies of God and the promises of Satan.

There are churches and ministries that proclaim that God is going to punish his chosen people (that is the Aryan race) and raise up the Edenites against them. One third will die from the sword and one third will be taken captive and the remainder will die of sickness. Do you really think that God is going to change sides and gang up with Satan against his chosen people? (This prophecy has already passed.) No, if man rejects God and worships Satan he must be prepared for the consequences. Is Abel-Sutt artful enough to psych us out with mental poisoning, making us believe it is Gods will, thus inevitable, and therefore we will succumb without a fight?

Before we can win a battle we must first identify the enemy. Think for a moment, is it in God's interest to destroy his people, is it Christ's teaching to destroy man and to damn nations? I don't think so! It is, however, the jealous God of the Old Testament and it is to Satan's or Abel-Sutt's advantage to destroy Adam Thor's Aryan Race and set up his Church as a world ruling power? Then history will repeat and nuclear war will result. The only alternative to war would be the suppression of man, another plunge into the dark ages of ignorance; stopping man from attaining knowledge which leads to his ultimate perfection.

El goes on to tell him where he comes from and his ancestry. Adam Thor doesn't need the Matriarch to tell him who he is or where he came from, but as he said he will just keep quiet and listen to what she says.

She tells him he is of the upper class and he comes from the west which is probably Atlantis, which is no doubt so far true. She can't help perverting it a little, claiming him to be a descendant of the wolf tribe and later claiming Abel to be a descendant of the Eagle; confusing the unsuspecting, making it difficult for them to distinguish the good from the bad or Cain from Abel.

Eldi the Hound of Eden quoths:

Thou art Ōttar born of Inn-Stone,
And Inn-Store was of Ālf named the Eagle,
And Ālf was of the Wolf-tribe, the Seafarer Wolves.
And the Seafarers were Swans the Red.
Thy mother, thy father worshipt as a jewel,
Methinks she was called Hlēdī, the priestess.
Frodi the prudent was her father, and Friaut her mother.
All that race ranks with the upper-class mankind.

Ali (thy great-grandfather) of yore was an awful strong
    man.
The first of the Dan region, he was far the highest seated
    of the young Shields.
Famous was his oar-pulling, in the folk-fights they waged,
Whereof his haughty work reached the skirts of heaven.
He allied with Eymund, a Western man,

Who slew Sigtr-Ygg with the swollen-edge (stone-club).
He owned a paramour Alm Veig of Western kin,
They had a race of eight sons.
These are the young Shields; these are the skilled ones,
Thence are the Oedl-ings; thence are the Yngl-ings,
Thence were the Land-holders borne, thence were the
    Hers (Aryans) borne,
The master-men and valiant under whom is the world—

All that race is thine! Ottar of the Homesteads!

She also tells Adam Thor of Eve's ancestry. She says she is
born of the sea, no doubt Atlantis, which no longer exists. Also
she is of the same royal Gothic blood line as Adam Thor. This
substantiates their race being the same as Adam's, as mentioned
earlier in the wedding scene.

Eve or Gunn's (Guen-Ever's) Ancestry

Eldi quoths: The ward Gunn-the-warrioress (Hildi-
    Gunn)—her mother was

The bairn of Svāvo and King Sae, sea king.
All that race is thine! Ottar of the Homesteads!
Verily none else wits so much! Wilt thou long for more?

She tells of Abel's ancestry, too, saying he is her sweetheart son, born from Wodan and herself.

Baldr, Abel or Ty's Ancestry

Eldi quoths: Herward, Hrans and (my) sweetheart Ty
    (Abel),
Bui and Brāmi, Barri and Reifnir,
Tind and Tyrfing and the twins Hadding—
These in the east Bolm (land) were born:
The sons of Arn-Grim (Wodan) and Eyf or Ur.
These Bear-sark brothers were the bulls of many queans,
O'er land and loch they regaed like lowes:
I ken both their broth and their skins,
They were of the herd of Hrolf of the Eagle,
All born from Iörmun the widow (me).

The Old Matriarch El prophesizes again. She tells Adam Thor he is a mighty ruler, but a mightier one will come although she cannot name him (most likely Cain). Then she says he must meet the Wolf Baldr Abel-Sutt and he will rip up Adam's rule of reason.

Adam Thor's Ancestry

Eldi quoths: O Sig-Urdar (Arthur?), son-in-law, list thou
    to my saying!
Grim folks were these and woe of Fāfni (Wodan-Abel).
But he (thou) the wise leader wast from the young Voels,
And his herd was from the young Reds (red-caps?)
And his loved leman (Eve) from the Oedl-ings.

All that race is thine! Ottar of the homesteads!

There was One (thou) born in the fullness of days,
Mighty, much eyed and of the ruler kind,
Newly born is he, this Peace-worshipping man.

He is of the Earth the Mighty Eye,
The swallow of the cool sea, the son of dreams.
Much have I said to thee; and I remember more:
Verily who else wits so much? Wilt thou long for it?

The Abyss will gang storming against (thy) Himin
   (Heaven) itself,
Gliding far o'er land, and the lift will open,
Thence from the Abyss comes the snowy one, the Snarer
   of Vinda.
Then is the redding up—the threat against the Reason-
   Rulers.

He is more than all of the born ones,
He is the mighty Eye of the Earth,
His (mere) word stills the stormy panics,
Sif's (Eve's) wedded Dan is he, with seat at Georgeville.

Then will come another and mightier one (Cain?)
Though ne'er can I name him.
Further now I do not long to see
Than that Od(-am)-o'-the'Inn must meet the Wolf (Baldr).

Hame ride thee Od(-am)-o'-the-Inn and shelter thy glory!
So come man no more after to visit (Eden),
Until Loki (Baldr) is let loose from his bonds,
And the ripping up of (thy) Reign of Reason comes!

She then goes on to tell Adam Thor that he has his eye on her
magic bowl. This magic bowl is the original of the witches cauldron
in the fairy tales. The cauldron where the evil witches brew up
their magic spells. Of course it is no more magic than a book of
do-it-yourself magic tricks, the tricks confound the spectator until
they look in the book and see how it's done. It's the same with
El's magic bowl. There is no such thing as magic, it just appears
that way. El confounds her people by keeping them in ignorance,
performing her wonders, mystifying them and keeping her knowledge a secret to herself. This same magic bowl or cauldron has
since been disclosed as the consecrated stone bowl of Eden. None

other than the much sought after Holy Grail of King Arthur and his Knights of the Round Table.

She also tells him that the Abyss will storm against heaven itself (Revelation 9:1). The coming of the holocaust. If this lay, as Cain is not mentioned, is out of sequence, this would refer to both the past destruction and the coming one.

Some churches claim prophecy to be dualism; an actual event at the time of recording and a prophecy of a similar event in the future. Hopefully, I can explain to the reader that not only is the story of man written in dualism, but it is continuous.

Firstly, it is a record of our God kings, our creators; carnate, in flesh and blood, living among us, their actual deeds, their day to day life, their accomplishments and civilization. It is all written and recorded. Man in the last three thousand years has relived the same chain of events, only each event stretched out into years to accomplish, instead of days; then the same events were lived again by the son of God in the flesh. Re-enacted, in symbolic form, the same events to remind us of our creator Adam Thor and rekindle the light of the truth which we had lost. We have about two thousand five hundred years to live out the life of Adam again. The sequence of events which we have to relive are layed out in the Edda from which the prophecies in the New Testament were taken.

King Arthur or Adam Thor, thought to be mythical, has been proven an actual human king by the recovery of the stone bowl of Eden that is El's magic bowl and consecrated as the Holy Grail of King Arthur (Adam Thor). It was inscribed by Adam Thor's great-grandson dedicating it to Adam Thor as his famous war trophy won from Eden.

If finding the Holy Grail buried in 3247 B.C. under the central sun tower one of the oldest sun temples in Mesopotomia at Nippur by the Pennsylvania Museum Expedition and inscribed as stated proves Adam Thor, our creator, to have been on this earth in human form, then it also proves that Eve and Cain were also here in human form and consequently Wodan, the Matriarch El, and Abel, also.

Just who is this mightier one that El is referring to? Is it Cain?

If so she still claims that the Wolf Baldr, or Abel, will conquer the world. Or is it Abel-Sutt himself who is going to be the mighty one?

Maybe we have a choice at this point, maybe this is the greatest election of rulers of all time. If we continue to go the way we are it looks like Abel will be the mighty one. If we wake up and turn ourselves around then it will be Cain.

Of course, we realize that Adam Thor only went to Eden to visit El to find out what their plans were. Now we have been forewarned, this is in no way a prophecy of God. This is a threat from Satan. He is dead serious, so fight we must; we can see the face of the enemy now, we can recognize him. He is the performer of magic, suppression, ignorance, bondage, superstition and deceit. (Rev. 12:09 The devil and Satan the deceiver of the whole world.)

Our weapons are freedom, truth, honesty, justice, morality and knowledge. We must get out from under this shroud of religious mystery and superstition which Abel-Sutt has cunningly wrapped around us like a spider wraps its victim in a shroud of silk before devouring. The very name of Adam's government—the Reign of Reason—is a government based on knowledge and reason, not fear and suppression based on perverted religion. The memory of the Inquisition and the Holy Crusades should still be in our minds.

The Militia Crucifera Evangelica was established. It was an organization dedicated to defend the much loved cross of the true religion of Adam Thor against the profaned use of the cross under which all manner of atrocities have been committed in the name of religion. These gallant loyal upholders of the Sun-Cross were known as Chevaliers. The original militia, formed in Palestine soon after the founding of the First Christian Church, was the inspiration to the Bards and poets to resurrect King Arthur and his Knights of the Round Table into the Christian era. Christianity was supposed to be a stepping stone to the return to Adam's solar worshipping cult, but through the suppression of the Catholic Church our founders of this earth and its civilization were reduced to myth and fairy tales.

In the next scene we will go even deeper into the perversions of our scriptures and our myths. The reasons why and how we know they have been perverted.

SCENE XVIII
LOKI VISITS AEGIS HALL

Loki, or Abel-Sutt, decided to visit Aegis Hall at Vidara, or the Gothic "Heaven" where Adam Thor and Eve lived with their Asas, or, as in the Arthur legends, King Arthur with Queen Guen-Ever hold court at Camelot with the Knights of the Round Table.

Loki or Baldr Quoths to Cook Outside Door of Banquet Hall

Say thou Cook! In thou shalt not go!
Afore thou gang'st another foot from me, say
What have the Aryas in the Inn been chattering on o'er their ale,
These "divine" sons of Sig?

Cook: Of their weapons, and Doom Law and compassion in
fight,
The divine sons of Sig quoth,
Asas and Alfs, the Aryas of the Inn;
But not one man o' them speaks aught a friendly word o' thee

L to Cook: In shall I gang into Aegis' Hall
And see the 'sembly about that.
Jol and Atta bitter spice, I bring the Asas' sons, To blend their
mead with venom.

Cook: Fetch thee they will, if in thou gang to Aegis' Hall
To see the 'sembly there,
Ruffian and rogue! If e'er thou go near the wholesome Regs
They maun wipe it off on thee!

L to Cook: Fetch thee cook will I, if thou scullery me
With one more sore scathing word,
Richly will I swear if thou say more!
          (Loki enters the Aegis' Banquet Hall)

L inside hall: Thirsty I come to this hall,
Lopt the Lion, from a long way.
Asas! I bid ye give to me one
Drink of your merry mead!
                    (No response)

L: Why tush are ye so? Ye throng of Goths!
And ne'er a word for mighty me?
Seat or standing will ye me at the 'sembly
Or bid me hence?

Gunn or Cain, as Master of the Feast:
Seat or standing at their 'sembly
The Asas ne'er will give thee!
The Asas well wit what 'sembly
The old skulking wolf-gammoner should get.

L to Thor: Mind thee Od o' the Inn that in days of yore.
We two blended blood together (in battle)?
Ale to pree, let thee hinder not a moment,
And seize a snug place for us together by the board!

Thor Adam to Cain: Rise thee Vidar let the Wolves' father
Sit at the 'sembly,
Lest aside Loki quoths his foul stuff
In Aegis' Hall

(Then says the text: "Then Vidar [Cain or Aegis] stood up and
    bore a cup to Loki, who before drinking, quoth to the Asas:")

L seating himself: Hail Asas! Hail Asa ladies!
And all the great holy Goths,
All save that one Asa on the inner seat,
That braggart bard on the bench (Gunn or Cain).

Cain conciliatingly to L: More (mead) and much will I give thee
    as my fare,
And better it to thee also with my own Baugi's poem,
So thou yield'st no offence to the Asas,
Nor grimly rousest the Goths against thee.

L or Abel to Cain: Ash-sticks and baugi-bangles are the arms
for minors, not of men.
Thou bench-sitting vain braggart,
Of Asas and Alfs inside here today,
Thou'rt the wariest of fight,
And the shyest of shooting.

Cain to L or Abel: I wit that if we were outside, and I was not
the 'sembly foreman,
And thou not a guest in Aegis' Hall,
Thy head I would have in my hand,
And let you have that little for thy lies.

L Abel to Cain: Snail'd art thou by sitting, skill'd art thou inside
your own George-town,
Braggart bench croucher!
Away thou cur, if frighten'd for thyself,
And think not for to fight for't.

Eve as Idun appealingly to Cain: I bid thee Bragi (Cain),
Sif's bairn duke
And well-wishing Maga (Michael)
That thou ire not at Loki's foul stuff
In (thy own) Aegis' Hall!

L to Eve: Tush thee Idun! Thou, quoth I, of all women
The very worst yearner after lust,
Since thou layest thy white arms
Around thy "brother's" bane (Adam).

Eve to L: Loki, quoth I, says foul stuff
In Aegis' Hall.

Eve to Cain: Bragi be calm, thou rich in beer!
I will thou wrangle not with him, nor fight!

Adam Thor to L: Erring art thou Loki and out of thy wits
That thou grimly mak'st a foe of Gefion (Eve),
Than the old warlock (Eldi), I think her more witted,
And quite even with myself.

L to Thor: Tush thee Od o' the Inn! Thou kennest thou ne'er
Dealt fights with fairness.
Oft gavest thou to them that were serfs,
And made slaves into seigneurs.

(Loki goes on to shower obscene abuse on Adam and Eve, till
the latter is roused to exclaim indignantly:)

Eve to Abel: Tush thee! If inside the family in Aegis' Hall
There was a son like (thee) Baldr!

Thou'd ne'er come out alive from the Asa sons,
For they'd verily slay thee in fair fight.

L Abel to Eve: Then as thou wilt Freyia, that I don't against
thee flare
More of my mean stuff,
I'll rid thee of myself. Thou'lt ride (in future) by thyself,
And (I) Baldr will sit in the cellar (of Hell).

(Here a stream of more foul abuse from Loki.)

Eve warns L Abel of disaster: Flapping is thy tongue, I guess
it's got the foremost of thee,
And tries to overawe me with yells.
Wroth with thee are the Asas! Wroth with thee is Asi of Ior!
Griev'd am I that home thou maun fare.
The Wolf (thou) I see lying afore the mouth of the River Ar,
Until thy ripping up by the Regis.
Thy moment is nigh unless thou now tush
Tongue-bound thou baleful smiter!

L to Thor: With gold thou boughtest Gymi's daughter (Eve),
And sold for her thy sword.
When Muspell (Hell's) sons ride o'er Murky Wood against thee,
Fetch thee then we shall, and swerve your way!

T to L: Ale'd art thou Loki and out of thy wits!
Why not loosen off Loki?
Thy overdrinking a wealth of old wine
Makes thee unmeasur'd and unmann'd.

L to T: Tush thee Home-daler! Thou wast (led by me) in early
  days
A hideous, restless, loathsome life (lying guarding the frontier),
With muddy back thou maun aye be,
And awake as warden of the Goths.

Skadi, Lady Asa: Let be thou Loki! Mind thee not for long
  thou'lt go
Larking loose-tailed.
For thee skulking Wolf in the rimey cold, Maga (Cain, Michael)
With gut-gear will bind goodly well.

(More abuse from Loki)

Eve forgivingly offers Abel a cup of wine:
Hail to thee now
Loki! And take this brimming chalice
Full of aged mead.
But let the one who holds it, with Asas' sons,
Be loosened from thy slander.

(It was all in vain, however, Loki's malignant and foul tongue
  could not be gagged, and it roused the long suffering Adam
  Thor to exclaim:)

T to L: Tush thou raging wight! Thou shalt (feel) Thrud's
  hammer
That mauler will knock thy malign speech afar:
Up will I warp thee to the East way,
And set thee down unmanly one sore.

L to T: Of East faring, thou should'st ne'er
Say any sayings for that,
Since thou wert (once there) knocked with my hand-thimble
  (wheel) O Einride!
And though'st not then thou wast Thor!
I quoth to the Asas and to the Asas' sons
That what I hugg'd in my mind,
But for thee only maun I outgang
For I wit that thou wilt fight.

(Loki Abel is led out of the "Heaven" of the Goths by Gunn
  [Cain] or Miok [Michael] whom he thus threatens:)

L Abel to Cain on expulsion: Ale brewest thou Aegis for
  the elder folk thou lik'st
To sit in the 'sembly under George,
But all the ale thou ownest, here in the Inn,
Loki's flame will lick afar
And burn they back!

Abel-Sutt's sole purpose of coming to Aegis Hall was to insult,
slander and malign the Holy Goths. First he insults Cain as a
braggard then he ridicules the Goths and calls them beardless
babes for going forth with the Rowan-ash Cross, instead of forcing
their way with the sword. He calls Eve a whore and goes on with
his insults saying Adam Thor bought her with money like a whore,
and is selling her favors to finance his campaigns, making him out
to be a pimp.

The Asas, prior to Abel-Sutt's visit, were discussing their laws
and how compassionate and just they were in fight. That is, they
only fight at the last resort. And also how they dealt with anyone
found guilty of breaking their code of ethics. These would be
judged fairly and punished accordingly. As Eve says to him after,
he has slandered and insulted them so badly, if you were one of
us, or if you were in our court, you would be judged fairly and put
to death.

Finally Cain gets fed up with him and throws him out of Aegis
Hall or "Heaven". On being thrown out Abel-Sutt is angry, he
swears that his flames will lick afar and burn their backs, in other
words he will continue to malign and slander the Goths.

This scene is very important, it warns us of what is to be
expected, that Abel, (his name means destroyer), will twist, malign
and pervert every move and every truth that is made or taught by
the true religion that is represented by the true original Rowan-
ash Cross. The belief that the sun is the sustainer of all life and it
is the true representative of the one God of Heaven.

(Reve 12:9–10 is the biblical version of Cain throwing Abel out
of Heaven. "And the great dragon was thrown down, that ancient

serpent, who is called the devil and satan, the deceiver of the whole world.") The only truth that Abel ever spoke that you can believe is his promise that he will deceive you.

Being forewarned of Abel's malicious intent, we can re-examine in a new light the first God of the Post-diluvian era and come to an understanding of how his legend became so perverted. His name was Adonis, Attis, Osiris, or Dionysus, depending on whether you are in Syria, Cypress, Phrygia, or Egypt. By some he is considered as separate individual Gods, of unrelated origin. By others he is suspected of being one God, worshipped by different people. Some think he is Satan and others a tree spirit and some a God representing the seasons of the year, dying in the winter and resurrected in spring and others would have him the God of the Harvest, and Aphrodite, his wife, a common whore. But, as we already know, they are Adam Thor and Eve. We will see how they got so perverted and confused.

Now remember that Abel said to Adam, "We blended blood together in battle." He also said, "Since thou were knocked with my hand thimble wheel O-Enride," reminding him that he was wounded by him once before and he intends to wound him again.

In the days after the destruction Adam re-established his one God, Sun-worship religion, again; and the process of uplifting man had begun all over again. Abel, as he promised, "Flames will lick afar, and burn they back!" starts maligning Adam and perverting man's mind with his lies. His first lie was that Adam Thor was dead when in fact Adam Thor was only wounded in the head quite seriously, but only wounded. Cain removed the missile with meticulous care from the wound and Adam recovered.

Symbolically this represents the death of the old world and a resurrection of a new world. Abel wasn't satisfied with just saying Adam was dead, but ground up and blown to the wind, making a resurrection impossible. Man, believing Adam was resurrected from the dead, was thus believing a lie which is the first step in Abel's strategy of undermining the true beliefs, as I explained previously. As with Adam as with Christ, both being Gods, were judged by man assuming the authority of God. A judged God, making it appear that God was judging and condemning God, causing Attis to say, "Dedicated to Odin, myself to myself." And also Abel makes Attis die by his own hands by having him castrate himself under a pine tree and bleeding to death. This is the source of the legend in the Bible of God destroying the earth himself, instead of man destroying the earth influenced by Abel Sutt. Adam Thor came to save Earth not to destroy it.

Abel further perverts and maligns the Holy Goths through their moral code, the Ten Commandments. The one in particular at this point is the fifth (page 99, *British Edda*), on sex. Abel has prevented this one knowing full well that sex and marriage are the center theme of the story of man, as mentioned earlier. God's wooing man with love and truth, when man submits to God's love and vows to be true to him alone. God then impregnates him with his Holy Spirit begatting a new life, the embryo of the spiritual man, the inner man.

This is demonstrated so we are aware and can understand the principal in the man-woman-husband-wife relationship. When woman submits to her lover she is impregnated by his seed which starts a new life within her.

Abel or Satan is also competing for the hand of Eve or, symbolically, mankind. Winning them over with the promise of anything which appeals to their vanity, greed, lusts and sensual pleasures. It is obvious to man that this way of life leads to sorrow and degeneracy. So Abel deceives man into believing all sex is sin. Man is conceived through fornication, therefore he is born in sin. Not distinguishing between sex in marriage as a beautiful thing, an act of love, a bond in marriage and the perpetuation of the race, and sex as lust and a sport which leads to degeneracy. Now he is saying sex is evil. The only way to become perfect is to abstain from all evil which includes sex.

So, blaming Adam for trying to educate and uplift the world, led to its destruction, claiming perfection is self-destructing. Now he relates the self-destructive force of attaining perfection to sex. Now if you aim for perfection you must be sinless, if sex is sin, you must abstain, if you abstain you leave no seed, no descendants, the human race becomes extinct.

Abel has twisted the legend of Attis castrating himself, trying to attain perfection, bleeding to death, thus hoping to deceive man into thinking that perfection is self-destructing, therefore unattainable. Thus, out of this confusion, this deception, this attempt of Abel to destroy Adam forever. Something beautiful bloomed, the symbol of love grew from blood which Adam shed on the ground from his wound inflicted by Abel. Love and truth still prevail and probably the origin of the rose and the cross, the emblem of the true religion of Adam Thor.

In the early days after the near complete destruction of the world and its regeneration by Adam Thor, it is obvious that the survivors knew that the world wasn't completely dead. It was, like Adam Thor, very seriously wounded; so it was in actual fact only a symbolic resurrection. The believers knew that, so they celebrated the event annually to keep them in constant remembrance of their past mistakes. The birth of the new sun right after the winter solstice symbolic of Adam Thor, the light of the new world. The death and resurrection at the spring equinox represented the death of the evil old world and the emergence of a pure sinless world from the ruins.

This was a sinless world for a period of time. As we saw in Scene XVI Adam Thor broke Abel-Sutt's arm, putting him out of commission for seven days (possibly 700 years). After Abel's arm healed he was back to his old tricks, deceiving man.

It was only those that listened to Abel-Sutt who believed that their God Adonis, Attis or Osiris, depending on the country, was completely dead and blown to the wind, making a resurrection impossible. Therefore founding their new conception of their belief or religion on a deception would lead to its further perversion. God made laws to be depended on, we base all our knowledge of science or anything for that matter on indisputable laws which are the same yesterday, today and tomorrow.

God set these laws in motion, we have to work by them and he has to abide by them, too. After all he created order not chaos. Everything works in harmony with the laws. Magic appears to be something apart from the law, but there is no such thing as magic; it just appears that way until we find out which laws are used and how they are applied.

Abel not only said Adam was dead but ground up and blown to the wind. Cut in half, cut up into fourteen pieces and scattered over Egypt. Nothing nor anyone that destroyed can be resurrected, it is contrary to the law. The only way would be to use new material and start building it from scratch. Using the original set of blueprints, is the closest thing possible to resurrection, which would be reincarnation.

Our genetic makeup is programmed so that our body can overcome disease, it can heal lacerations from surgery or accident, it can knit broken bones and can even absorb unnatural growths and tumors back into the system and eliminate them. Faith healing is known to be a positive factor in overcoming any of these conditions because it is beneficially programmed in our genetic makeup. But it doesn't matter how much you pray or what you think, if you cut your arm or head off you will not grow another one, because you are not genetically programmed that way.

A good yardstick by which to measure our advancement is by the amount of magic we still believe. Abel-Sutt, having worked deception into religion, found it quite easy to further his plan of take-over by appealing to man's reasoning and his basic nature. If celibacy led to the extinction of the race, to assure propagation of the race the worship of sex was introduced. This, appealing to man's lusts, was readily accepted. Young maidens were given to this Mother Goddess, the personification of all the reproductive energies of nature, to prostitute themselves for money in the temples in the service of the Goddess, Mary Cybele Artemis or Astarte; the proceeds going to maintain the temple. On the festive days all women were required to shave their heads, those who refused to give up their locks had to give themselves to a stranger. The cult of Cybele was led by Eunich priests, dedicated to her service. Their orgastic rites celebrated with frenzied music of flutes, drums and cymbals, excited the emotions of some of the spectators to where they would grab a knife and unman themselves on the spot dedicating themselves to the services of Cybele. You can see how craftily Abel-Sutt has turned their faith to the worship of the Matriarch El in practice and to Adam Thor and Eve in name only, thus making Eve appear as a whore and a mother of harlots, true to his maligning insults at Aegis Hall. This insult also applies to Adam Thor where he says, "With gold thou bought Gymi's daughter (Eve) and sold her for thy sword." It is not hard to understand how this came about—look at our temples of today, our T.V.s and movie screens. It is the norm, not the exception, that our women indulge in free sex. If this isn't becoming the worship of sex what is it? And who is it that is influencing us? Abel claims that Adam bought Eve's favors like a whore, and sold her favors for money to further his cause.

For further study on these Gods I found J. G. Frazer's *The Golden Bough* to be of great value in documenting the historical facts, and his detailed account of the rituals and traditions of these myths has made it possible for me to further construct my theory, but I differ with his conclusions.

SCENE XIX
THE BINDING OF LOKI-BALDR BY CAIN

Garm Wolf curses Miok
Afore the Gnipa (rocks o') Hell.
Fastenings maun be slitten
When Freki (Baldr) runs (again).

Fetter'd she sees lying
Under in the Ewer Grove,
The lie-yearning Liki,
Loki the evil thoughted.

But they know Vala's (Baldr's)
Victor's bonds to snap,
Holding him so hard,
Those stubborn bonds.

There sits the Si(n) queen (El)
Beside the unloosed sinews
O' her wily paramour, godless.

Know ye yet the Edda?
Know ye yet it all?

Apparently Michael has Abel-Sutt bound. I don't see too much importance to this lay as he doesn't seem to have done anything since he had his arm broken, except visit Aegis Hall and insult the Goths. There is a little conflicting thought in Scene Eighteen. According to what I am using Cain just threatened Abel-Sutt. "And thou not a guest in Elgis Hall, thy head would I have in my hand."

In other accounts of later Arthur legends (Cain) Sir Gawain cuts off the head of the Green man or Black Knight (Abel-Sutt) and he takes off carrying his head in his hand, suggesting that it is not possible to kill Satan thus he re-appears or is re-incarnated as Abel-Seth, Cain's younger brother as portrayed in the Old Testament.

It seems that this lay could be the first slaying of Abel-Sutt. he is thus bound hand and foot until such time as he is freed in the form of Abel-Seth.

SCENE XX
ABDUCTION AND RAPE OF ASI SIF OR EVE
BY BALDR OR ABEL SETH

Skulker (Bald) is named the wolf,
Who follows the baptized Gothess,
Into safeguard Vidar (Ptteria):
Even another Hate,
He, the son of the Riotous (old) Wolf,
Shall fare away with the bright bride of Heaven.

Then go the Regis all
To their rock-stools (in parliament)
The great holy Goths
And counselt together on that:
Where are the lewd traitors
Who have caused this lofty loss?
And given the maid of Od (-am)
To the race of the Edenites?

Thor alone rose there,
Thronged in burning mood;
He seldom sits
When suchlike things are asked:
Oaths were gone against
And the sworn words,
All the main treaties
Between both sides betrayed!

Thor quoths: "I see for Baldr,
The bloody Tivo,
Wodan's bairn
A warlock felon's fate!
The stud-bred waxer of the Inn
The Sibyl of the Harri (Aryans),
Fine and mickle fair (was she)
As a mistletoe tine!
The ward of them is maimed,
My fine one sinned against!
The hateful harmer
Will Hod (-am) seize and shoot!"

Thus Baldr's "brother" warned:
Bor-o'-the-Inn soon warned (that)
He'd so seize Wodan's son
In one night's fight:
That he'd neither wash his hands,
Nor kem his hair,
Before 'gainst Bāl in battle,
As Baldr's enemy, he'd be.
And Frigg grat o'er it
In the cellars of Fen,
On the woes of Val's Hall

Know ye yet the Edda?
Know ye yet it all?

After Abel-Sutt has been freed from his bonds he follows the Goths to their capital and as you notice "even another hate" under another name. He is now Seth, he abducts Eve and carries her back to Eden. This is an actual happening but it is symbolized as the abduction and rape of the religion. As we are aware woman is synonymous with church or religion, so Seth abducted Eve in person, in actual fact, but symbolically he abducted the religion as he promised in Scene XVIII. Phrygia, a stronghold of the Goth Sun-Cult of Adam Thor, was where this abduction and rape occurred. Having perverted the legend of Adam Thor under the name of Attis, having castrated himself trying to attain perfection.

He further defiled the religion by replacing Eve with the Matriarch Mother Mary under the name Cybele, a Goddess with a face of black jagged rock. The festivities of these orgastic rites were celebrated from the 25th to the 27th of March. Included in the festivities was a sacramental meal and a baptism of blood. The devotees would descend into a pit over which would be placed a wooden grid over which a bull would be led and then stabbed to death with a spear, its hot blood gushing forth, pouring down through the grid, drenching the devotees in its scarlet blood. The bull represented the dying God Abel-Sutt, whom Cain had slain, baptizing the initiate into the cult of the worship of the Matriarch Mary, or Cybele, in the blood of Satan (Abel-Sutt), accusing Cain of slaying righteous Abel.

Fig. 26—Mithra (as Cain or Michael-Tascio) slaying the demon Bull. From marble sculpture in British Museum. Note the young hero with Phrygian cap of Liberty, Ears of Wheat (for starving aborigines) issue from the death-wound. An attendant bears the Fire-torch of the Sun-cult. The Bull is defended by the Wolf, Scorpion and Serpent. (After *British Edda*, L.A. Waddell.)

Thus constituting the rape of Eve and the abduction and rape of Adam's Solar Cult. This provoked Adam, Cain and the Holy Goths into action which we will see in the next scene.

SCENE XXI
CRUSADE OF KING ADAM-GEORGE AND CAIN FOR THE RESCUE OF EVE FROM ABEL IN EDEN

Fig. 27—Thor and Cain (*Āmo* or Mioek, *i.e.,* Michael) received in Eden by the abducted Eve. From Hittite seal, *c.* 2000 B.C. Note all the details exactly as described in Edda. Oku-Thor is stepping down from mountains with his hammer, Sun-Hawk, and in front of his foot his handled Cross; and the Sumer sign in front of him reads Uku-shu (*i.e.,* his Sumerian title of *Ukusi* or *Agushi*.) Cain or Āmo bears his Sumerian name-sign *Āma* (a wild Ox-herd); and Eve or Asi (bearing her Sumerian name of *Asha*) is holding out a cup of wine. On the left is the Bowl or "Ewer" cauldron, which is filling the cups of the two sitters. (After *British Edda,* L.A. Waddell.)

Then were the He-Goats out o'home for the rake,
Speeding with poles, swift the duteous ones ran.
Rocks were riven by Odo, earth burnt aflame
As Od-o'-the-Inn's sons (drove down) to Eden-Hame.

Flying was the pedestall'd Rood at the Red Fell
Afore Ot (-am) the Goth. At the whetting
Of the Dragon Lopt, against that liar,
Lower'd was its rope by Home (-dale) Father.

This Rowan-goad (oracularly) quoths: "The green
Goths' Her-Thrum beaten track,
Verily there the true way for
The steed of George-the-Red lies (to Eden or Carchemish)."

The Goad of Strength then Thor lets go
Down (the trail) of the lewd Gamms (Vultures)
Where the fey (serpent's) tusks and thrusting horns
Of sic nether folk abide.

There wended George geared with the disc,
A-shooting the wicked Gandrs richly,
Ending ne'er until (he reached) Ymi's Land,
Ida's seat from Thridia (Thor's capital Vidara).

George the Warden in faring forth so far,
Swore to maim the noxious harmer,
To scathe and bind with one swoop,
Saying "The Galdrs (Chaldees) and rogues!
I'll make Grim's Gallman (Ty)
The betrayer, holler a grand stream (of song)!
I'll open the evil gapes
Of the Endils with my spoon!

And the gone Vans in going,
Those war-wolves, have torn from (my) heaven
Frida, her husband's, that foremost of matrons,
Sorely come to dreary dregs.
But I'll break the baleful quother,
The braggart Loki, the villain:
My broidering wand (will ply) on the back
O' the son of the brothel 'brides,' the sedge sows!"

Athwart his way, the weir-bridge had vanished:
Its feet, the swinish nuns, and
Its hilt, had haggl'd and halted him;

But he leapt the river o'er the gaping weir.
Miok the (men's) leader ne'er staying leaped
Like their stick-leader. Thus the broad way
O' the Urd River was thrust past,
Then the adder's eastern Thiod River snorted in rage.

There in the murky forest afore the marches,
Bur (Adam) hastily sitting said:
"Not the revolving wheel (stone-mace) here
Has scotched the Adder (River) into suavity—
That knotted, ragin, hacking, freezing one—
But the Wood (Cross) measured the wrestling splash:
That (it was) which fell'd the running stream
And fell Fedio, and made (its barrage) stop."

Hard wax'd the Nar (River) letting up to his shoulders,
With his heels on its bed in such flowing.
In this gateway of mud, Niotr (Thor)
Neatly (an end of) his niard girdle far (flinging),
Athwart let it twirl to be seized by
Thor's bairn, who was hisself merry
And smart, tho' blotted up to the neck.
Yet still the stream waxed more.

Ōdo (Adam) steadfast, but his friend afloat,
Swore (by the Rowan) the oath of the Goths.
"Seats for the voyagers may the sapient sword Rowan
Gain (for us) in the fens,
Tardy the running waves harden the earth!"
The Rowan quick the needed
Earth supplied: A snow-bridge (it became)
By the appled-ash of the blazing red wood.

Unto its midst, out he heaved himself,
By the Apple-Rowan that was his shield.
And clinging to the belt of Heaven's siōla (king)
Came safely leaping out Thi-alfi (Thiazi, Cain);
For 'twas Ado and not the reckoning Mimi (nimi, Cain)
Who strode the stream alone.
Then ne'er stopp'd they afore the stepped
Into the strife-laden vale of the Grids.

No more deep (flooded) acres dripped across
To the devilish weems of these weres of gloom.
Striding on, talking without standing still,
The pedestalled Wood-bearer rushing fell.
Awestruck Diar (Thor) fain the lots (would see)
But his son (Cain) on the firth hugging merry baths (quoths:)
"The spill of the Wood isn't to be feared:
Thor and Thi-alf are as strong as stone!"

Then (Thor) girded with his companion at his side,
They let out their swords against the hateful ones.
Shielded by the Wood-board, they warred against
The horde hard yelling their war din.
Afore the Hell-rider, the Red Rood,
Heide's heathens fled in fear from Ōdar the divine.
The bright Wood-shield (Rowan-Cross) shot
The squealling heathen wreakers.

> *Know ye yet the Edda?*
> *Know ye yet it all?*

We have already found that Adam, as George-the-Red, is the historical original of St. George of the Red Cross of Cappadocia, now patron saint of England. His red cross being discovered in my former work to be emblematic of the sun, which he worshipped as the chief source of life in the world. (page 148, British Edda.)

Adam Thor takes up his standard and the pedestalled Red Cross accompanied by Cain and his faithful upstanding Goths, which are symbolized as He-Goats. The goat being the emblem of the Aryans, or Goths, which is the Sumerian name for Goat, versus the lion, wolf and serpent emblem of the Edenites or Wodanists.

Outraged by the abduction of Eve, which was actually the rape of the Solar Cult, Adam Thor and Cain, "The herder of the He-Goats," set out to rescue Eve under the protection of the Red Cross or Rowan Cross or the Apple Ash of the blazing wood, the true Golden Bough. Adam Thor and Cain seem to arrive ahead of their men. This fact is quite significant, as when we relate this event to this present day we will see that Cain or St. Michael is way out ahead of the rest of his men in the rescue of Eve and hopefully, this will help speed up his men so they are with him in time to do battle.

As they strode forward, striding across mountains, rivers parted and became dryland before the invincible Rowan Cross, their faith was their strength. It is important to notice that Moses used his staff of Rowan Ash to part the waters of the Red Sea, the same as Adam Thor had parted the waters of the flooding rivers on his crusade to rescue Eve and to save mankind from the clutches of Abel-Seth which was the first crusade of all. Was Moses wise enough to know Satan would pervert his record of the past, so he left a clue that we might understand at a later date, when knowledge is increased and freedom prevails, that the Israelites left Egypt on a crusade to save mankind again from Satan? And not as a tribe of Hebrew slaves running away in fear from their oppressors.

Could the drowning of the Egyptians in the Red Sea be symbolic of the end of an era? The symbolic transfer of authority from the Pharaoh's to this present day Aryan leadership? There is another such event in our ancient history which might possibly be associated with Melchezedek, King of Salem, priest of God most high, and Abram at the Valley of Shaveh (The Kings Valley) in Gen 14:17. And King Tarsi "divine" and his famous victory over ten confederated Kings about 2900 B.C. His miraculous crossing of the flooded Parushni River (Euphrates) and the returning waters drowned most of his pursuing enemies. (Page 171, Makers of Civilization.) Could all these miraculous water crossings each be symbolically representative of a crusade? Jesus walking on the water re-enacting the crusade which Adam had led? We can see in Matt. 14:28–32 a parallel between Adam Thor and Cain to Jesus and Peter. Cain clung to Adam Thor's belt and was pulled safely from the waters. Peter caught Jesus' hand and was thus also safely pulled from the waters.

SCENE XXII
RESCUE OF EVE BY ADAM THOR FROM ABEL IN EDEN AND PUNISHMENT OF ABEL

Striking confirmation of the authenticity of this Eddic record is found in the ancient Hittite seal of probably about 2500 B.C. in which the rescue of Eve by Adam is depicted in all its details precisely as preserved in this Edda. Adam Thor is portrayed girdled, stepping over mountains and entering the Eden abode with uplifted club (or hammer) in his right hand and grasping the fruited Rowan Cross in his left hand, with his symbol of the eight-rayed Sun in front of him. The imprisoned Eve is seen of white complexion holding up her skirts, and above her left hand is the Cross of Adam, with the crescent Moon underneath to indicate that Eve was originally of the Lunar cult. Prostrate below her is Abel as "The Steer of Eden," with his Wolf-head and Vulture symbols. Behind is the Matriarch El of Eden, crowned, with her hands uplifted in supplication, with her Lion (or Wolf) and coiled Serpent symbols and two attendant weirds. Here again the remarkable and literal historical authenticity of the Edda is established. (page 158, *British Edda*.)

> Driving 'midst the drifting knavish devils,
> So the divine Ōdar surged up,
> To Sōt he fared afloat, who fled to his door
> Where Ivo (Eve) was nested.

Fig. 28—Adam's rescue of Eve from Abel in Eden with Rowan-tree emblem. From Hittite seal of probably about 2500 B.C. For description, see text. (After *British Edda*, L.A. Waddell.)

Then the Fire-wrester, the fast flood-riving
Dāni (Dar-Danos) stood—
The knocker-down of Ioln's (Helen's) race stood—
Afore that out-hustl'd lout.
They were (twain), the doughty (Cross) bearer, Thor,
And Ran's hugging bairn:
That limmer warden of Hell who came howling,
Baulked from going:
That lustful father was fast held,
And Frid (Eve) was there inviolate:
Snibb'd was the lady against the gripper,
And there rested the green-hatted queen.

Ok's (Thor's) hammer on Logi humm'd hail
It humm'd on the filbert of Vall
The Truth-Ash wood trod down the Moony
Form brow to sole, thwacking
The hooded steer, on the path,
Where raged the hovering hitting twain.
The laughing Ell-Ida, Hell's foremost hound,
The Kiaol woman (quoth):

"Fetch away betide thy seiz'd Froedi from Eplis' (Abel's)
    firth!"
Quoth the Queen of the Earth,
"With me she lay, not with the mob of (harem) women,
And all is right, I ken.

The elm tie-ropes are loos'd (off her):
Aegir (Aegil, Abel) the angry-thief, slic'd the thongs.
Now Od-o'-the Inn's awful seething with the nether race
In the South should be gone!"

So At (-am) for (further) shindy rapping,
Not minded to swill for (further) fight,
He lifted the brooch'd one from the Lion's too long
    friendship,
And so thronged forth.

Then is The Thrasher of Ur with the Asa Esio (Asi-Eve)
Out from Hrimni's floor of dross,
And away from the throes of the moody dark brides,
The weirds of the Gripper's breast.

> *Know ye yet the Edda?*
> *Know ye yet it all?*

This is the actual rescue of Eve, and also the symbolic rescue of Adam's Sun Cult, the keepers of the true faith, who had not succumbed to the perversions and deceptions of Abel-Seth. This again is parpled in the Old Testament. (Gen 18:22)

Abraham pleading for Sodom and Gomorrah. I believe Abraham is the all wise dwarf of the Edda who had fallen in love with the Gothic maiden when Adam Thor was away. Symbolically, we can look at it this way, the all wise dwarf had fallen in love with the truth, he had searched out the truth and found it in Adam's Sun Cult even when Adam was absent. It was a Godless world at the time when Sodom and Gomorrah flourished. He said he didn't want to live in the darkness of Eden's cellars. He said he would sooner be dead than live without the truth and the light, or without that milk white maiden. Whether Sarah was a Gothic maiden I can't say, but she was reported to be very beautiful, quite possibly she was. But most important, All Wise had searched on his own free will and found a glimmer of light. Abraham was pleading for the Edenites' sake that Sodom should be spared. Adam Thor and Cain in those days could use force to rescue Eve because she had been abducted and raped. She would gladly leave with her rescuers no matter what they had to do to secure her rescue. But it is different today in that she left Adam Thor after her first born and chose to go to Abel-Seth, her lover. She even had children from him. If Adam Thor and Cain use force to get Eve back and wound her lover it will raise her antipathy and she will cling ever closer to her lover. So this time around we have to woo her back with love.

We can identify Sodom and Gomorrah with the Matriarch, the great mother goddess of fertility. When Lot and his wife and two daughters were rescued from Sodom, Lot's wife looked back. That of course means she didn't really want to leave that way of life, so she was turned into the symbol of what she represented, a pillar of salt. A white pyramid or cone was the archaic shape of the image of that ancient Mother Goddess. Gen 19:22—Make haste, escape therefore I can do nothing till you arrive. Therefore the name of the city was called Zoar. The sun had risen on the earth when Lot came to Zoar.

This doesn't mean that they had travelled all night to get there before Sodom was destroyed. What it does mean is that the light of truth had spread all over the earth and only those who rejected it were destroyed. As the cycles go around this light becomes dim and has to be rekindled as today the light is almost out again. We are waiting for another lamp lighter to appear and spread the light of truth around the world as the sun shines its light from the east to the west and only then will it be the time of the end.

For what it is worth you may use the same system of calculating as the religious groups have in the past to calculate the time of the end. That is using seven as a complete number, six working days and the seventh as the Sabbath, six thousand years and one thousand millenium. So by dead reckoning from the time of the beginning, according to the ages of the sages in the Bible, we are at the six thousandth year now. So far all the predictions have been wrong. But if you look at it from where I sit, the first recorded date in history is 3378. If 7000 years is allotted to us and if Jesus was crucified half way through the seven day week, if his ministry ended half way through a seven year cycle, if his crucifixion was in his thirty-fifth year, half way through a seventy year life span, then it is only logical to assume that he would have started his ministry half way through the 7000 year period, which would be 3500 years.

This would allow Christ to be thirty-two years old before he started his ministry. That would be 3410 years, ninety years short of the 3500. I can't arbitrarily insert ninety years to make it right, but I can look into the eastern branch of the Aryan race and see how their dates work out. The eastern branch was responsible for the civilization of India, China, Mongolia and Japan. On looking into China we find that when Jesuit missionaries first arrived in

China they found, to their amazement, in the ancient Chinese archives an account of Lao-Tsze, a God begetting a God on this earth 3468 B.C. If you like to add the thirty-two years to this number you can arrive at exactly 3500 years. So according to that we have 550 years left before the end of time. But it is all of no account for as Jesus says if those days had not been shortened there would be no flesh saved alive, so those days will be shortened. By how much? One year? One hundred years? Five hundred years? We still don't know, only God knows. All we know is that the light of truth will shine all over the world before the end comes. I can't even see across the street, but then again it may be my eyes.

The sun had risen and its light had shone on the Earth, including Sodom and Gomorrah, by the time Lot had arrived at Zoar. I am not criticizing what one believes. If one doesn't know one has to believe something, but when it is proven right or wrong the wise retain the truth and discard the false. When the light begins to shine are you going to be like Lot's son-in-law to be and think it's a joke?

SCENE XXIII
CAPTURE OF THE MAGIC BOWL OR HOLY GRAIL OR MOUNTAIN STONE OF EDEN BY KING-THOR AND ITS CONSECRATION TO THE SUN CULT

Then the holy beef-dish (bowl) o' the hall,
The Head o' the Hawks (Cain) comes to broider.
Under in the flat it was broiling,
Fornenst the feet of the Thrasi witches;
This tidbit of Gull, Ullar (Cain) loos'd
In the teeth of the three tied witches,
Those nether maimers amid their mess,
And he dirl'd out the beaker (afore) their nose.

Gloomy aneath in their armed gear,
Grumbling with drenched skins
O'er the vanished cellar-song (bowl) of Victory
They louted on the hearth beaten.

At the coming of the two, Vidar (Cain and) Mit-the-divine,
The ale can they saw harmed,
Let out on the path, the metal brimmed beaker
Fallen and Eden wrecked.

The Hell-blood sacrificer woefully nipt,
Hack'd and broken in the shaws—
Under the fell attack of young Alf o' the Hames,
That bright blinking calf.
No (more) folk-feasts from that lost crafty cheerer,
The meet wishing-bowl of the matron;
The old mind-can is down,
The fiery stone of Ell, the trickster!

This scene, again, is of the greatest importance. The basis of
this theory rests on the understanding of the true identity of the
Holy Grail. What it was, why it was broken and why it was buried
by Adam Thor's great grandson, Udu or Uduk, in about 3242 B.C.
beneath the foundations of the central tower of the oldest known
sun temple in Mesopotamia at Nippur. This scene appears to
equate with the Biblical legend of the Tower of Babel. The reason
King Udu buried the stone bowl beneath the sun temple at Nippur
with the inscriptions of the first four Aryan kings dedicating it to
his great-grandfather, King Thor or King Arthur as the original of
the famous vanished war trophy, the magical stone bowl or caldron, captured from the Matriarch El at the well of Urd in Eden
by Her-Thor (as revealed in the Edda) was to establish beyond
doubt the indisputable proof at a later date, which is now in this
generation, that the account preserved in the Edda is the true
history and prophecy of this world; dating back to 3378 B.C. and
that Adam Thor, King Her-Thor, Ar-Thur, Zagg or Pur Sakh with
his wife Queen Gwen-Everor Eve and their son Cain, Kon, Gawain or Michael were the actual human originals of the Arthur
legends. King Arthur, Queen Gwen-Ever, Sir Gawain, and Abel
(not the younger brother of Cain but as Abel-Seth or the Green
Man or Sir Lancelot of the Arthur legends); the son of the arch
enemy of Adam, the evil human and animal sacrificing mother-
son cult of Eden; the Matriarch El or Morgan Le Fay, and her

consort Wodan and son Loki Baldr or Abel Seth, the deceiver of the whole world. The suppressor of mankind, the Eden triad. There is proof that the legends of King Arthur were resurrected into the post Christian era at the time of the renaissance with the hope of re-establishing the true faith, which was thwarted by Abel-Seth discrediting their validity, reducing them to mere myth and fairy tales.

The much sought after and cherished war trophy, the Holy Grail of the Arthur legends, has lain buried and forgotten; being lost for over five thousand years; and has led to speculation of its identity from the womb of Mary Magdalen to the cup that Christ's blood was caught in to the wine chalice which Christ drank from at the last supper. We now have the actual fragments of the stone bowl of Eden as the consecrated Holy Grail (page 174, Plate XXII, *British Edda*) exhumed from beneath the central tower of the oldest sun temple at Nippur by the Pennsylvania Museum Expedition sometime around the turn of the century (with the oldest known historical inscription in the world, page 88, *Makers of Civilization*).

Consecration of Eden Bowl by King Her-Thor as "The Holy Grail"

Now have you heard how the Ewer-Can was worn like
    that,
As the Goth artists carve with such skill;
That Ewer of the Earth Ruiner he fetched as a loan,
Thus both he, the Chaldee (Eve) and the bairn forged forth
    to their own.

One may wonder why in the ancient seals we are always reminded that Eve was originally of the moon cult of the Caldees. The fact is we must not lose sight of who she is. Eve, or the woman who married Adam, is representative of the Church or congregation, which is Mankind. Mankind was created by God, therefore man's ancestry goes back to God. Eve, or Mankind, chose to follow the Matriarch and Abel then denounced them and Eve married God, swore to be faithful to him and bore a son to him. Abel, by deception, abducted Eve, or Mankind, and stole her

THE CONSECRATED STONE BOWL OF EDEN AS "THE HOLY GRAIL" OF KING ARTHUR.

Fig. 29—*A.* The Stone Bowl fragments bearing the original archaic Sumerian inscription of Thor's great-grandson, *c.* 3247 B.C., in burying the trophy, and unearthed below foundations of central tower of the oldest Sun-temple in Mesopotamia, at Nippur, by the Pennsylvania Museum Expedition. *B.* Suggested restoration of Bowl or Grail. (After *British Edda,* L.A. Waddell.)

EVE OR IFO, GUNN-IFO OR GUEN-EVER, AS SERPENT-
PRIESTESS OF EDEN BEFORE MARRIAGE WITH KING
HER-THOR, ARTHUR OR ADAM.

Fig. 30—Ivory statuette, *c.* (?) 2700 B.C., 6½ inches high, in Art Museum, Boston. Provenance unknown. Been supposed to be Cretan, but flounced dress is typically Sumerian and Hittite, and figurine suggests figures on old Gothic cathedrals.

Sumerian Lists.			Indian Lists.	Nordic Eddas.
Udu's Bowl.	Kish Chronicle.	Old Sumerian List. (See Table opp. p. 140.)		
SAGG or Sa-ga-ga (or SAKH) (or INDARA)	UKUSI of Uku	AGUSHE-ir or SAGKI	IKSH-VĀKU, SAKKO or INDRA	OKU or SIG or ANDVARA, EIN-DRI
GIN the established (son?)	AZAG, BAKUS or BASAM	GAN, GUN or KAN s. of 1	AYUS or BASU or BIKUKSHI, s. of 1	ÆGIS or BAUGE, GUNN or KON, s. of 1
ENUZUZU or IN-ZUZU, s. of 2	NAKSHA, ANENUZU, s. of 2	IN, ENU, UNNUSHA	NAHUSHA, ANENAS or JANAK, s. of 2	HŒNI
UDU or UTU, UDUK, s. of 3.	Devotee of King SAGG or Sa-ga-ga.	(U)-DUKU	UDA of the Vase, s. of 3, or YADU or YA-YATI.	

Bowl Genealogy compared with First Four Kings of Sumerians and Early Aryans.

away. God is rescuing Eve; or Mankind, his wife; with the help of Cain, who is rescuing his mother. His mother is Eve, or Mankind, the Caldee or Semitic people of the world. Cain is represented as the brotherhood of righteous men of Aryan Stock. The product of the marriage of God and Mankind. He is the begotten son of God born of Mankind, the Son of God.

> The doughty able Ug (Thor) came to the Thing of the
>   Goths
> Wearing thus on his head the family Ewer of Hymi.
> Then Veor shall drink well from that Ewer
> Ale of the Deer at Aegis' Hall, each Harvest-tide.
>
> > *Know ye yet the Edda?*
> > *Know ye yet it all?*

Fig. 31—King Her-Thor or Ar-Thur carrying off the Eden Magic Bowl on his head as a Hat. From Hittite stele trophy from Birejik, now in British Museum. (After *British Edda,* L.A. Waddell.)

This sacred trophy stone bowl of the first Sumerian King Ukusi or Dur (or Tur) is inscribed and dedicated to the latter by his great-grandson King Udu of Kish City, the fourth imperial king of the first Aryan Dynasty. It is now disclosed as the actual original material of the famous war trophy, magical stone bowl or caldron, captured from the weirds at the well of Urd (Urudu) by Her-Thor as detailed in the Eddas. As further proof only fragments of the stone bowl were found beneath the sun temple, as this coincides with the breaking of the bowl at the time of its capture, which has a profound symbolic meaning in itself.

Now we can ask ourselves what was this stone bowl? Why was it sought after and when won, why broken? Why worn as a crown by Adam Thor or King Arthur?

This stone bowl has been revealed as the magic bowl of the Edenites whereby the Matriarch El could foretell the future and know the past, and was able to perform mysterious wonders. In our fairy tales it is portrayed as the evil witches caldron used for brewing up evil spells. We realize now that magic only appears that way. It is typical of the Edenites to suppress knowledge and to mystify their subjects. By keeping them in ignorance, they could maintain power. That stone bowl was in fact, their well of knowledge. The key needed to decipher all the accumulated knowledge of the past civilization which, as I am suggesting, was contained in their time capsule or great pyramid built by the people before the flood or great destruction. The Edenites were in possession of this key, the stone bowl; or, as sometimes referred to, the mountain stone, which is quite suggestive of the pyramid itself by shape and enormousness of structure.

Adam Thor knew the nature of the Edenites. He knew that as they relearned the secrets of science and the knowledge contained in the pyramids with the use of the key to the universal hiero-glyphic picture language they would only use it for evil and it would be but a short time until they were in a position to destroy the world again.

The capture of the stone bowl was a much celebrated event, but to ensure the Edenites didn't regain it, it had to be destroyed. Both Adam Thor and Cain are seen in the Edda trying to break the bowl but to no avail. Finally Eve knowing the Matriarch,

Fig. 32—Hitto-Syrian Ceremonial Chair of fifteenth century B.C., presumably used by the high priest at the Bowl or Grail festival. Found in tomb of the Hittite high priest, who was the grandfather of King Akhenaten, the Sun-worshipping Hitto-Egyptian king of Egypt. Note the Goat (Goth) adoring the handled Sun-Cross (triplicated), surmounting the Bowl. (After *British Edda*, L.A. Waddell.)

suggested Cain should smash it over El's head as that was the hardest thing there.

> In the days of yore Val Tiva came spying,
> And in the 'sembly slowly afore saying a word,
> He shook (his divining) twigs to see the lots,
> To find there at Aegis' Hall the ordeal cheer in the Ewer.

> There sat the Hill-dweller (Cain), the tidy bairn, in front

> Miok—much blind to such like,
> Who looking in the eyes of Ygg's bairn (Cain), in thrawn
>   (mood) quoth:
> "Thou oft has a 'sembly for the Asas geared!"
> That fate-working Edenite, the word-badgering tailed
>   (wolf),

Hugging (the notion) of being in Heavendom next to the
   Goths,
He bids Sif's husband hisself fetch the Ewer (saying):
"Then I'll tell ye all o'er your ale of a heater (Toddy-
   bowl):

"None can match that of Maid Mary (El) and Tiva,
And the great Regis can get such nowhere!
'Tis the one of (all) truce-cups of Ty (To) Hlōrrida,
Easter's foresight is most in that sage one:

Afore the byre (it stands), east of Eli of the waves,
At the hound-wise witch Hymi's, at the end of heaven.
At my mother's moody kettle,
That roomy brewing Ewer, is the deep of rest.
Feast ye will if ye get that lucky well,
If thy wily friend will let it with its gear!"

(So now) they (Thor and Cain) had driven forth thither for
   days
From Asgard until they came to Egil's:
The Herdsman (and) the He-goat of the horned gos-hawk,
And hurried into the hall in Hymi's hut.

Moeg, the snow-White Āmo Mioek led in himself,
Hefty-headed as nine hundred (men)
Then another (Eve) jogged forth all golden (haired),
White-brow'd, the bearer of the beer wassail herself.

Eve quoths: That kinswoman of the Nether Edenites
   (quoth), "Well (glad) am I to see ye!
Full of hugs (am I) for ye twa! Sit under the Ewer
Which my 'friend' (Abel) marks himself
Glegly with guests. For George he hugs ill-will!"

Still wet was that tyrant, warder of that seed-spell abode,
The hard tyrant (of) Hymi, home from the hunt,
Jogging into his cellar, gloomy and icy
Was the churl, when in came the shaggy kin of Frae (Eve)
   of the Inn.

Quoth Eve outside to Baldr: "Were thee keep hale,
Hymi (bolt!). Inside are the hugging Goths!
Now is (my) son come into thy cellar,
He whom I've waited for, from a long way,
And following him Her Ōdr, And the Skoti,
The Friend of Man, who Vēor is hight.
Beware where they sit under the cellar gable.
So forth save thyself: stand afore the pillar!"

But sunder'd was the stock of the pillar afore the sight of
   the Edenites,
'Twas already in twain, broken by the Asas,
And the stock of eight (Ewers), only one of them
Hard sledged remained whole.
Forth came they (Asas), but the old Edenite
With loathing eyes for And-Skoti
Said to herself: "Mind well when thou seest
Him that makes witches weep, come in on thy floor."

"There (also) is Thjora (Taur, Cain), the taker of the three
   (witches),
Both of them going after the Eden seether!
Where don't they lift their heads shameless?
And at (my) fireside sitting bravely!

And that Edenite, unfriendly as ever,
In throes of spite and taunting Thor,
Quoth she: "Ramming strong men tho' ye be, Roa and
   Kynni,
Ee'n with thy crafty might yel'll ne'er break my chalice!"

Then Hlo-the-Rider (Cain) came at it with his hands
To let break and burst the broth-stone glari,
Sitting agog he slogg'd it on the pillar,
But it was borne black whole from Hymi's skirts.

Until Frida, knowing that harlot
Easter's foreknowledge, the mikle wisdom of the adder
   (quoth),

"Das it on the head of Hymi, that is harder,
Than every choice meat-chalice of Eden!''

Then the hardy He-Goat guardsman, rising from the
    knees,
Brought the dish with all his Asa might
Down upon the helmet-head of the churlish Hell
    enchantress,
Then the round wine-carrier was riven (in cracks).

Mary quoth: "I see my meet treasure gone from me!
I see my chalice in knocking ruined!''
Quoth she, that churl: "Never more can I say (to that
    one)
After this in my life: 'Ale art thou heated?'

That one thing so choice (I doubt) if I can mend;
Out thro' mine own fury goes the ale-keel of my house!''
Ty looking on, Ty swearing at the ruin,
Stood beside the other. The Ewer rested calm in front.

Then Father Mōda fetched it from the snakes,
And in going striding o'er the floor o' that nether cellar,
Sif's husband heaved up upon his head the Ewer,
As a holy trophy enringing his skull.

Symbolically breaking it over her head suggests complete destruction, even to the point of knocking what knowledge she had
of it out of her head. Now the key to the secrets of the great
pyramid has been destroyed, it is no wonder that they have stood
as a mystery confounding man for so many thousands of years.

It is quite evident that the Holy Grail is the equivalent of
enlightenment and knowledge as we see its symbolic effect on
different periods throughout history. It very well could be the key
to the pyramids as we see King Thor winning the Grail from the
Edenites and breaking it over the head of the Matriarch, putting
an end to the evil use of knowledge that they were acquiring from
the possession of the bowl. It was the key needed to unlock the
knowledge stored in the great pyramid from the previous civilization. Consecrating the Grail, sanctifying all knowledge as the

holy and righteous truths of creation and the cosmos. Symbolically crowning the Kings with the Holy Grail, trusting to them the awesome responsibility of using this knowledge for the uplifting and betterment of mankind with the aid of the Asas and a select group of honest, trustworthy, loyal and righteous Aryan men and women, the high priests of that day which formed the sworn brotherhood which was known as the Great White Brotherhood.

As we see through history there is a succession of battles fought, battles won and battles lost. As we see when the Edenites were in control, Adam Thor's code of ethics were being eroded away, morals were slipping, education was coming to a standstill, knowledge was decreasing, a dark age of savagery was on them, and man was living in superstition, fear and ignorance. The Matriarch's and Abel-Seth's way of ruling the creation, the monsters they had created. It is Abel-Seth's belief that if man, the creation, is allowed his freedom to accumulate knowledge he will become unmanageable and be a threat to his creator. A theme used in many of our science fiction novels. Adam Thor on the other hand argues that man is created in the image of God, therefore if given his freedom of choice and all knowledge is made available to him he will eventually become perfect; then he will be one of them, perfect in his thought, offering no threat. That, oversimplified as it may be is, in a nut shell, what the battle between the Edenites and Aryan Goths is all about. Suppression of knowledge versus the expansion of knowledge. When Adam Thor and Cain won the Grail light shone on Earth and knowledge expanded.

At the end of Sargon the Great Dynasty, 2521 B.C. Abel again managed to seize control. The second Enech dynasty, a weak Sumerian dynasty, plunged the Sumerian civilization into one of the darkest periods in Mesopotamian history. This dynasty was short lived, only a matter of about twenty-six years, and was followed by the Guti or Gothic dynasty from 2495 to 2360 B.C. which was considered the Golden Age or the Sumerian Renaissance.

We find, by the beginning of the Guti dynasty, that the Holy Grail had been lost for about 1000 years. By then a quest for the Holy Grail had started. It was an age of enlightenment and knowledge was increasing again. There appeared a new Holy Grail in

King Gudia's reign, a substitute for the lost original one, and it was offered to the deified capturer of the original stone bowl of Eden. "St. Michael, the Archangel of Heaven and vanquisher of the Dragon (page 31, *Makers of Civilization).*

Fig. 33—The intertwined Serpents on a Sumerian votive stone-bowl or vase dedicated to Lord Mukhla or "St. Michael," the canonized second Sumerian King, by King Gudia about 2370 B.C. Note the Dragons on either side protecting the double Serpent. (After *Makers of Civilization,* L.A. Waddell.)

This period was not what is referred to as the end time knowledge explosion as the original Grail was still lost. This apparently was a substitute Grail which was the result of the sincere effort of the first Avitar or Grand Master of the Brotherhood, the inspiration behind Buddhism. (Gautama is only the last Buddha dating back to around the late sixth century B.C., there have been others before him.)

This period was short lived, however. We have an amazing parallel here with that of Jesus, the next Great Avitar to appear in the world. The Grand Master Jesus came to enlighten the world and lead mankind back to the truth, to the original ways and beliefs as taught by Adam Thor. There appeared another Holy Grail at that time. It was the sacred cup used by Jesus Christ at the last supper. It was preserved by Joseph of Arimathea who collected in it the blood from the body of Christ. This Grail, too, was still a duplicate or symbol of the original. This again was to be lost, the original had still not been found.

The Sumerian Renaissance was short lived. The Grail, the light which Gudia had brought (in the form of Buddah, the first Avitar), was compromised by the following Ur Dynasty, 2350–2200 B.C. They embraced wholeheartedly, for the purpose of gaining popularity, the aboriginal Moon Cult of his Chaldee and Semitic subjects with its debasing animal and human sacrifices and the immolation of wives at the burial of their husband. Thus compromising the Avitar's teaching with the Edenite Cult led by Abel-Seth, raising to first cast the Brahman's whose priests declared themselves direct descendants of the Lord God and that they were of divine origin and twice born (page 387, *Makers of Civilization*). Then came the slaughter. Purash-Sin, the establisher of Brahman's as first caste, led crusades destroying all the Sun Cult worshippers who were considered enemies of the Brahmans, even including the slaying of his own mother who was a follower of the Solar Cult (page 397, *Makers of Civilization*).

Fig. 34—Parashu-Rām as Purash-Sin I exterminating the Kings who opposed the Brahmans. In this Indian art we see Purash-Sin I brandishing an axe, thus equating him with Abel-Seth. (After *Makers of Civilization*, L.A. Waddell.)

Thus the commencement of another dark age. Comparing this with the other duplicate Grail of Jesus Christ we can't help but see a striking parallel. Jesus brought light into a Godless world of confusion, a new era of truth and knowledge, Christianity had taken hold. A new era of enlightenment was beginning, but only to be short lived as what appeared to be another compromise was about to take place.

It seems the Semitic Chalden religion of Rome swept down on Christianity, destroying all the original manuscripts, editing and selecting from all the writings only that which would fit into their own religion, popularizing it to accommodate the masses and compromising the truth. Then the crusades started again, martyring all the true believers in the name of Christ and declaring them to be the enemy of the newly formed Catholic church. Thus a new dark age had begun, the Grail was lost.

You may ask, where was the Brotherhood at that time, why didn't they come forward and say that Christ's life was only a re-enactment of Adam Thor's life and that Christ didn't die the same as Adam Thor didn't die? They, of all people, should know no faith can stand on a deception. There was no deception among the true Christians. They knew Christ was not dead, they tried to tell the world that. They were martyred and burned at the stake for doing so and were labeled heretics.

Now how can I start to explain the master plan which has been told to us twice symbolically which we still fail to understand? Whether this plan was in effect in Gudia's time, the inspiration of Buddhism, I can't say; but there is a plan and it is going according to schedule for us today. Until we know what this plan is there is nothing much we can do wittingly to hinder or help it.

To start to get a mental picture of the plan we could first look at the mighty cedar tree. Cedars grow out of the dead rotten stump of cedars that have died. If we imagine a big old rotten dead stump of a cedar and a little seedling about three inches high and as big around as a pencil planted on this rotten stump, and it takes root and sends its roots down all through that rotten stump and it grows. When that beautiful, live, green tree is fully grown it will have consumed that rotten stump and not a trace of it will be found anywhere. In its place will be a beautiful live green tree. Now we see the principal of the plan. We will now see how it's put into practice. First of all, we must bear in mind that these facts are extremely important, namely—the virgin had to be named Mary, Christ had to be crucified on the cross, Christ did not marry in his lifetime, Christ is dedicated to marry the church (his mother?) or Mary Magdalene.

The Virgin Mary became a Vestal Priestess of the temple at three years of age until her thirteenth birthday. She married God and bore a son. She later married Joseph and bore more children, and Joseph died. As I pointed out the parallels in a previous scene between the life of the Virgin Mary and Eve. That was the first time the plan was revealed to us; we didn't understand it then, so it was revealed to us a second time by the re-enactment of Adam Thor's life by Jesus and St. Michael or Cain. It still wasn't understood. Hopefully, I can explain it in plain simple language that anyone can understand.

This is a combined effort, it is masterminded by Adam Thor and put into practice on Earth by Cain or St. Michael. St. Michael is very real, if you pinched him he would holler. The plan is to plant this little cedar seedling firmly on that old, dead, rotten cedar stump, nurture it so it will take root and grow.

Firstly, a High Priest of the Temple of Helious by the name of Joachim had a daughter born to his wife Anna. The High Priest's of the brotherhood, knowing she was divinely ordained as was predicted, said she had to be named Mary and she was dedicated to the temple. She was taken to the temple periodically by her mother. At the age of three she voluntarily stayed in the temple and became a vestal or virgin of the temple until her thirteenth birthday. Now the brotherhood, we won't call him Cain or St. Michael we will refer to him as the Brotherhood, had their virgin. They knew by the signs that the re-enactment of Adam's life could begin.

At the age of thirteen Mary was given the choice of either staying in the temple or leaving it in the guardianship of one named Joseph. He is acting the part of Abel-Seth, he is identified as being a carpenter and having an axe equating him with Abel or Satan.

She was courted by both Abel and Adam, she chose Adam as Eve did. Then came the immaculate conception, which I might suggest here as being an artificial insemination of Adam's seed by a being from heaven, unknown to Mary that it would cause her to become pregnant. After she bore Jesus she then married Joseph, who we saw was playing the part of Abel, and had more children by him.

We see in Scene XII after Eve is married to Adam she becomes his Priestess. She scales out the Baptist's mead (the wine that never wanes), and we also see her teaching Cain the Ten Commandments. The Church or congregation is synonymous with woman, and woman is synonymous with Church or congregation. It is the same way for Mary, she will be referred to as the Church, religion, cult or doctrine.

We also see that both Marys, the Virgin Mary and Mary Magdalene, were present when Jesus was taken from the cross, that both Marys were the first to go to the tomb and that both Marys were the first to see Christ after rising from the tomb. It is hard to explain the two Marys but it is important that there are two Marys. You see it wasn't Adam's mother that Abel abducted and raped, it was Eve his wife. Jesus wasn't married but he is betrothed to the Church and he will marry the Church, that makes him marry his mother. He doesn't in reality it just has to appear that way. If he did marry his mother it would be incest. It just appears that way to equate with the Matriarch Mary and her lover-son Abel of the Romish Temple. In fact he will marry Mary Magdalene. Mary Magdalene is his lover who came running to him when he was wounded which equates with Aphrodite running back to her wounded Adonis (Adam).

Of course Mary Magdalene equates with the Christian Church. The true Christians, the Sun Cult of Adam, came running back to the old faith at the wounding of Christ. The blood from Aphrodite's feet which stained the white roses red equates with the blood of the martyrs of the early Christian Church spilled by the Edenites of the Romish Church.

We must remember that time doesn't mean any definite time period but the amount of time is important, *e.g.* one day can equal one year, seven days can equal seven thousand years, three years can equal three hundred years, ten years can equal one thousand years. Now at this point Christ has been crucified and the revived Sun Cult has taken hold. It is doubtful if they call themselves Christians, they are growing and gaining strength but they are a worry and a concern to Abel and his Romish religion. He martyrs them and tries to suppress them, blood is shed continuously.

Now the plan is to plant that little cedar seedling into that old rotten stump. Of course we realize that the cedar seedling is the young Christian Church and the old rotten stump is Abel and the Matriarch Mary's Romish religion. As Adam's betrothed wife was a vestal of the temple at three years of age until her thirteenth birthday, so will it be for the second Adam, or Jesus, symbolically. Mary Magdalene was the body of the Christian Church. She was betrothed to Christ therefore, symbolically, she will be a vestal priestess of the Matriarch and Abel's Romish religion, the same as Eve was.

The Christian Church symbolized Mary Magdalene as voluntarily entering the Romish Church as a vestal virgin during the rule of Constantine I in about 325 A.D., three years equals three hundred years and allowing thirty-two years from before Christ's ministry it works out almost exactly to three hundred years. It is possible that Constantine I might have been of the Brotherhood. Now we have the seedling planted and we must let it grow for one thousand years, equaling the ten years the Virgin Mary served in the temple. It appears that Mary Magdalene's (symbolizing the vestal priestess/the Christian Church which was declared the official religion of Rome by Constantine I in 325 A.D.) time was up around 1332 A.D., at which time she left the Church accompanied by; as in Eve's case Abel Sutt and in Virgin Mary's case Joseph playing the part of Abel; Antipope Benedict XIII at the time of the great schism, 1328–1423. She symbolically married Christ and bore a son, Cain or Michael, symbolized by the phenomenon of the Renaissance. Antipope Benedict XIII wooed her back into the Catholic Church. There she had other children by Abel who were half-brothers to St. Michael who are symbolically represented by the protestant denominations, offshoots of the marriage of Mary and Abel.

As we saw in the Edda, Abel-Seth abducted and raped Eve, or symbolically the Solar Cult, there were no children though. Adam and Cain stormed down into Eden, spoiling for battle to rescue Eve; in her case being abducted and raped against her will she gladly left with her rescuers. In this case it is a little different. Mary went to Abel of her own free will, we can't rescue her by force, we have to woo her back with love. Now, the way we are wooing her is very subtle. As it was in the Edda, Adam and Cain were way out in front of their men. If we can realize that they need our help, and we hurry up and catch up to them we can no doubt make the rescue a lot easier and sooner. Our weapons are truth, love and honesty, once we know the truth we must act on it.

The subtle part of the plan of rescue goes like this. Each ritual or rite that was celebrated or worshipped by the Matriarch Mary and her lover-son Abel and their Romish Religion, has a counterpart in the Christian Church. The Romish Religion for centuries before Christianity worshipped the Mother Goddess of fertility and her lover-son. With the roots of Christianity planted firmly in the heart of the Romish Church by Constantine I as the official religion of the Roman Empire has changed its name to Roman Catholic Church and the Mother Mary and lover Son whom they worshipped has been replaced by the Virgin Mary, the Mother of Christ. They have changed from worshipping Satan to worshipping Christ without knowing it or losing face. If the Virgin Mary had not been named Mary, but say Betty instead, this subtle change could not have been effected. (It is very important that we get the matter of Mary straight. All told there were three Mary's: The first Mary equates with Matriarch Mary or El. The second Mary is the Virgin Mary—the mother of Christ. The third Mary equates with Mary Magdalene, the lover of Christ. Each is symbolic with the Church—woman being church. The Mother Matriarch El/Mary needs no obvious explanation as this character has been previously described by the Edda's. The Virgin Mary, however, is Eve. Eve being the wife/lover of Adam Thor and the mother of Christ is symbolic of man's love for his church/mother. Mary Magdalene was the lover of Christ—not his mother—who was Virgin Mary. This again is showing the equation between woman and church, woman/man = love and church/man = love. There were two Marys, not one, at Christ's graveside. Mary Magdalene and Virgin Mary—not one woman as some believed but two very separate individuals—mother and lover.)

Celibate or eunuch Priests and shaven headed nuns were the priests and priestesses of the Goddess of Fertility, Cybele, from antiquity the same Mother-Son cult. Christ however, was not married but betrothed to Mary Magdalene or symbolically betrothed to the Church. The priests and nuns of the Catholic Church, subtly unknown to them, are still practicing their old rites and rituals. They have been turned around and are now dedicated to the Christian Church, as Christ married the Church in the early fourteenth century and begat a son who's symbolically Cain or Michael personified as the founders of the Renaissance. It appears now, in this light, that the controversy over whether Catholic priests should be allowed to marry may be resolved.

The black beads which the priests of the Matriarch used to help them memorize their chants have been very subtly changed to roses for their rosary and they don't chant in Latin anymore. They are speaking in a language which can be understood by the congregation, not confounding them anymore.

The cross was never a symbol of the Romish Religion but it was very artfully introduced to them. It was required that Christ be crucified on the sacred pine of the Edenites with his arm stretched out. That is why the Pharisees didn't stone him, as was their custom; he had to be crucified by the Edenites or Romans. Thus Abel gladly accepted the crucifix to profane the cross with Christ our Saviour, his enemy dead, nailed fast to its beam, like Prometheus staked and bound in purgatory forever. Our job is to proclaim the truth, get Christ off that crucifix and replace him with a rose. Then it will be the true Sun Cross and we will have rescued Mary, or the Church, back to Christ. There will be no vestige then of that old Mother-Son cult to be found. Satan will have been vanquished and the mighty hand of Cain will have slain the bull. When it is revealed that the Virgin Mary, the Mother of Christ, is *not* the symbol of the Church but that it is Mary Magdalene, the lover of Christ, they will understand and accept it. The final point is that Joseph died. When the church returns to Christ, or Adam, and the office for the head of the Romish church becomes vacant who will there be to fill it?

It is also interesting to note the parallels which run through the themes of our myths and legends. It is the same story, a beautiful woman abducted away from her husband, raped and the ensuing battle to win her back.

First we have the abduction of Eve, and the subsequent adventure of Adam Thor and Cain into Eden to rescue her. This also symbolized the rape of Adam Thor's Solar religion; that is, mankind's abduction into Abel's or Satan's false religion. Then we have the Biblical story of Sodom and Gomorrah where Satan had seduced mankind away from God's religion of truth to his false evil ways. The rescue of Lot and his daughters, the only righteous ones in the city, who became the Moabites and Ammonites.

Next, we have the Trojan war. Helen of Troy, the most beautiful woman on Earth, formerly a Trojan princess, left Troy to marry Menelaus, King of Sparta. This of course equates with Eve leaving Eden, the Matriarch and Abel to marry Adam Thor. Paris, the Son of King Priam of Troy went to Sparta and abducted Helen away from Menelaus and brought her back to Troy. This was the cause of the ten year Trojan War. Agamemnon, King of Mycenae, to avenge the wrong done to King Menelaus amassed an army to rescue his wife, Helen. The siege of Troy lasted for nine whole years, in the tenth year it was decided that the war could not be won from without, so a method was devised to gain entry into Troy so they could fight from within. The means by which they gained entry is well known in Greek legend. A huge hollow wooden horse was used by the Greeks to hide Menelaus and his warrior heroes. A Greek spy within the city of Troy convinced the Trojans that by bringing the horse into the city it would make Troy invulnerable. On gaining entry to Troy the Greeks leaped out of the horse, threw open the gates, letting the rest of the army in, bringing to an end the ten year war with the sacking of Troy. That was around 1200 B.C., which is substantiated by the burned ruins of the seventh rebuilding of Troy. The original city of Troy dates back to over 3000 years B.C.

In this story, which is part legend and part fact, Paris is obviously a prototype of Satan or Abel Seth. Helen of Troy equates with Eve, symbolizing mankind seduced away from God. Menelaus, King of Spartan, equating Adam Thor. Was Constantine the first, the spy within; and could Christianity be our Trojan horse?

At the time of the burning of Troy very few Trojans managed to escape. Aeneas, however, was one of the more fortunate. He, along with his aged father and young son, managed to escape aboard a ship. After sailing for ten years around the Mediterranean Sea they reached Italy at the mouth of the Tiber. There he was received hospitably by Lateinos, King of Latium. Aeneas later married King Lateinos' daughter Lavinia, thus founding the Roman race.

It appears that the Brotherhood doesn't want mankind to lose track of Abel's or Satan's whereabouts. It is recorded for future understanding in Revelations 13:18 "This calls for wisdom, let him who has understanding reckon the number of the beast, for it is a human number, its number is six hundred and sixty six." According to a publication by "The World Wide Church of God," *Who Is The Beast?*

The sum total of the Greek letter numerals contained in the name "Lateinos" totals 666; it signifies "Latin Man" and in Greek "Roman". Count the numbers: L = 30, A = 1, T = 300, E = 5, I = 10, N = 50, O = 70, S = 200.

The capture and the breaking of the stone bowl of Eden equates with Gen 11:5—And the Lord came down to see the City and the Tower, which the sons of men had built. And the Lord said, Behold they are one people and they have all one language; and this is only the beginning of what they will do; and nothing that they propose to do will now be impossible for them. Come let us go down and confuse their language that they may not understand one another's speech.

Confounding their tongue had the same effect on the Edenites as destroying their stone bowl, their source of knowledge. The United States of America, the greatest nation in the world, is a nation comprised of every race and color on Earth living side by side under one government with one language. It is not perfect yet but the time will come. No leader with any wisdom whatsoever would introduce bilingualism or multi-bilingualism in that great country. The result would be division and confusion and they would leave off building their tower. Furthermore, any race that would want to force their tongue on all the other races would demonstrate their selfishness and lack of patriotism.

After Adam and Cain had won the stone bowl of Eden and smashed it over El's head, even destroying the memory of the knowledge they had gained and putting a stop to the evil use to which they were putting their knowledge. Adam then wore it on his head as a crown, symbolizing that the dispensing of knowledge would be entrusted only to kings and high priests of the Aryan race.

Consecrating the stone bowl of Eden as the Holy Grail of King Adam Thor, changing it from its evil use to good righteous use. Knowledge isn't evil, only the use to which it is applied is good or evil. Consecrating it as holy symbolized that knowledge was to be used only for the betterment of mankind and not his destruction. Thus entrusted to Adam Thor and the Asas of his court, founding the Great White Brotherhood. The keepers of the secrets of the Holy Grail. Its foundation dates back to the beginning of the post-diluvian world. (Reference to sworn Brotherhood, page 282, *British Edda*.)

Now we have, in my belief, discovered who the keepers of the secrets of the Holy Grail are, we find they are a select few endowed with the responsibility of dispensing knowledge and maintaining the truth. King Arthur, St. Michael and the Knights of the Round Table; the Aryan race; sent for the purpose of befriending, teaching and uplifting man. They were once again in charge, the process of civilization was to start all over again.

This time, though, the knowledge was to be entrusted only to a few with the highest integrity of the Aryan race; namely St. Michael or the Kings and high priests sworn to secrecy not to divulge any knowledge to anyone other than the initiated students of the order. Most of the secrets were passed from mouth to ear. Written records were no doubt kept on some matters as they became more widely taught and applied in the daily lives of man.

The more profound secrets were not written as time passed. With successive generations the details required for the application of advanced knowledge became vague and eventually forgotten leaving only the germ of the idea, only the knowledge of it having once existed.

These germs of ideas have intrigued the minds of the great men. The masters and initiates of the Brotherhood, this secret order, down through the ages, reconstructed bit by bit these fragments of ideas. Like a jig saw puzzle the more knowledge that's put together, the faster the rest falls into place. As is prophesied in the Bible, at the end of time knowledge will be increased (as happened with the recovery of the original bowl, the Holy Grail, around 1900 A.D.). What happened to the Brotherhood, and who and where is the Aryan race?

As early as about 3100 B.C. the Aryan's vast empire centered in Mesopotamia, held as a colony the Indus Valley. (Page 27, *Makers of Civilization*.) Ruins of ancient Sumerian cities have been discovered in the Indus Valley dating back to that time.

The Guti or Gothic dynasty from 2493 B.C. to 2360 B.C. restored to what has been considered by Assyriologists as the Golden Age. "But their kings being overzealous in their religion subordinated their temporal governments to the priesthood spending their resources of their empire on great temples and supporting hordes of priests, consequently weakening their military might." (Page 385, *Makers of Civilization*.) This constituted a flagrant transgression of the Code of duty and ethics imparted by the Aryan Sage Aurva, or Grand Master of the Great White Brotherhood, around 2725 B.C.

This code holds as true today as it did in those days. The Sumerian Gothic or Aryan race has the divine purpose of being the civilizers, educators and uplifters of man, endowed on them by Adam Thor and guided by St. Michael and the loftiest minds of the sworn brotherhood.

The advice to kings is, "The ruler should cheerfully give presents to the priests, perform the sacrifices and study the scriptures. His especial source of maintenance are arms, and the protection of the earth. The guardianship of the earth is his, especial province.

By intimidating the bad and cherishing the good, the Monarch maintains discipline and secures whatever region he desires." (Page 211, *Makers of Civilization*.)

By not complying with the advice given above, the Gutti dynasty became weak and vulnerable to men of baser nature, which in this instance was the usurper Ulukegal of Erech, making the cleavage between Eastern, or Oriental, and the Western branch of civilization even wider. This led to further Semitism and Orientalist decadence of the following Ur dynasty. Who, in order to gain popularity, compromised their divine rights and embraced wholeheartedly the aboriginal Moon Cult of their Caldee and Semitic subjects, with its debasing animal and human sacrifices.

This Alliance of the Sun Cult with the Moon Cult or Serpent worshipping Edenites debased and perverted Adam Thor's Sun religion to the point where the world's first Avatar Buddah is reduced to an idol.

The Western branch of this Aryan World empire moved their capital from Mesopotamia to Egypt commencing with Sargon the First's grandfather, the first of the predynastic Pharaoh's. Sargon's father was overthrown by the usurper Zaggisi, 2750 B.C. Sargon, being a posthumous son never knowing his father, has a very similar experience as Moses some 1400 years later. Sargon was found as a small baby floating in the river in a basket made of bull rushes. He was found by an Aryan Sage, the fire priest Aurva. He was raised and tutored by the priest, no doubt master of the Brotherhood, in the duties of a ruler or king. This code of ethics and duty parallels Adam Thor's ten commandments and the whole of the ethical portions of the Mosaic code with the exception of the Jewish jealous God's sacred Sabbath or Saturday.

The code reads like this—"The Sun Lord is most pleased with him who does good to others; who never utters calumny or untruth; who never covets another's wife or another's wealth; who bears ill will to no one; who neither beats nor slays any living thing; who is ever diligent in the service of God; who is ever desirous of the welfare of all creatures, of his children and of his own soul; whose heart derives no pleasure from the passions of lust and hatred. The man who conforms to these duties is he who best worships the Sun Lord." (Page 210, *Makers of Civilization*.)

There must be a reason for these two great men to have started life abandoned to the river in bull rush baskets. In Moses' case he was found by the Pharaoh of Egypt and educated by the Brotherhood at Heliopolis. By this time, in Pharaoh Amenhotep IV's rule, the Great White Brotherhood was known as the Brethren of the Rose Cross. This beginning must mean the beginning of a new dynasty or a new leader unadulterated, unbiased by the world or his past. Raised and educated by the purest and most righteous and dedicated master of the Brotherhood to regenerate the faith which had been eroded by time and worldy ambitions.

Now we can presume that Moses, a Grand Master of the Brotherhood, is credited with compiling the first five books of the Bible. As we saw in Scene XVIII Loki Baldr or Abel-Seth is true to his word. He has perverted and maligned Moses right from the start. Adam is portrayed as a weakling, led astray by Eve his wife, and Cain the murderer of his brother. Abel has elevated himself to righteous Abel sacrificing a goat equaling a Goth to his jealous God, a Semetic version of the one father God of the Aryans. It takes little reasoning to understand that this is the work of Abel-Seth; the deceiver of the whole world.

It is irrational to think that Moses—having attained the highest degree in the Great White Brotherhood to the honor of Grand Master, the keeper of the secrets of the Holy Grail with the knowledge of the history of the Brotherhood—would malign Adam Thor, the founder, in such a fashion. At the time of the destruction of Sodom and Gomorrah, Abel-Seth had successfully deceived Adam Thor's Sun-worshipping cult in that part of the world and won them back to the old Edenite religion of blood sacrifices, fornication, and orgies; a complete degeneracy.

Abram on the other hand, had chosen to live outside of the city in the hills away from the degeneracy of Sodom and Gommorrah. Even though it was a Godless world, Abram searched out the truth and found his God. As the all wise dwarf he found his milk white maiden. Because of Abram's faith an umpire before his time (all wise). Adam chose to raise up an Aryan race from this Semite, a converted Edenite. Of course Abram was Semitic, so there was no way an Aryan or Gothic race could spring from him; but Adam Thor did give him a son, he gave him complete charge of raising and teaching this son.

We must not lose sight of the fact that Abraham was of the aboriginal Semitic race not having any of the Gothic characteristics in his makeup. He was limited in his comprehension and the Wodanist traditions of his past were still in his memory. To establish this new Gothic race the first miraculous conception was about to happen. By using our twentieth century understanding we could very well see that this conception could have been an artificial insemination performed by the said Angel's from a semen bank from their homeland. Abram and Sarah of course had no idea of what was happening so it was recorded in Gen 21:01: "The Lord visited Sarah as he had said and the Lord did to Sarah as he had promised and she conceived."

Now Sarah has born a son, Isaac (an Aryan or Goth). Abel-Seth, or Satan of the Bible, hears of this and immediately recognizes him as his competitor. He concentrates his attention on maligning and discrediting Abraham and his descendants as recorded in the Bible.

If we look at Gen 15:12–15 it might have read like this before Satan perverted it. "Then the Lord said to Abraham 'Know of a surety that your descendants will be sojourners in a land that is not their own and will be uplifted and taught the secrets of this world for four hundred years and they will come out a much wiser and enriched people.'"

Gen 22 could have read like this—"Satan, knowing Isaac a Goth, a son of God, was angry, so he appeared to Abraham as an Angel of light, appealing to Abraham's old traditions of human and animal sacrifices of his old Edenite religion. He told Abraham he would be pleasing his God if he would offer his only son Isaac as a burned offering to him. Abraham almost succumbed to his conniving deceptions but realized at the last minute that there was no light in it and it was a plot by Satan to destroy Isaac, a Son of God, before he could become a great nation and pose a bigger threat to him. Abraham did, however, revert to the old custom of blood sacrifices by sacrificing a ram which was equal to killing a Goth or a God in effigy.

Then later, instead of making plain what was obviously being done, that God was establishing a pure Aryan blood line through Isaac's descendants, only choosing and using the purest blood. But Satan makes Jacob to be a swindler and liar. Defrauding Esau out of his birthright by wearing a goat skin and deceiving Isaac, who by this time was blind, and Isaac bestowed Esau's blessing on Jacob instead, and furthermore makes God of Heaven condone this fraud and bless him.

Next we see Joseph sold into bondage in Egypt. In a very short time he becomes second-in-command to the Pharoah of the ruling Aryan, cast over the Semitic aboriginal Egyptians.

Joseph later married the priest of On's daughter of the Aryan race and decidedly not Egyptian. No doubt this Priest Potiphera was one of the Fraters of the great White Brotherhood.

Joseph's wife bore him twin sons, Ephraim and Manasseh. These twin sons could be almost full blood, main line Aryan's; possibly traceable back to Adam Thor's court. When Jacob blessed his sons as the twelve tribes of Israel this was symbolizing that these twelve tribes of Israel had the responsibility of continuing Adam Thor's task of civilizing and uplifting mankind the world over. Joseph and his sons were to become two great nations, Great Britain and the United States. Zebulun will become the Phoenicians, the greatest seafaring people of the world. Juda is to become a rich people binding his foal to the vine, and his ass's colt to the choice vine. The vine is the house of Israel and the choice vine is no doubt, through Joseph's line, the United States of America (Ephraim). This means they will have close ties with Britain and America. Suggested reading. *The United States and Britain in Prophecy,* published by the Worldwide Church of God. The rest of the tribes were to be distributed throughout the world.

The whole purpose of this was the Aryan influence was to be distributed through the world, civilizing and uplifting the aboriginal Semitic races. Like everything else it was frustrated by Abel-Seth. We realize the nature of man, we see it even in the animal world and in our children, in nations and even in the people whom Adam Thor chose to do his work on Earth. A half trained animal is dangerous, it neither fears you nor respects you, it is unpredictable, it will turn on you, when it is fully trained it respects you and is trustworthy. When children are little they worship their mothers and fathers; when they are half grown, half educated, they rebel, they think they know more than their parents, they say, "What do they know? They don't understand—we know it all!" With nations throughout history, uncivilized and underdeveloped countries welcome the Aryan influence but when they are half civilized they rebel, they think they know it all, they accuse their benefactors of exploiting them. The same thing with the people whom God chose to do his work; when they became half enlightened they rebelled, too; turning their backs on their creators, thinking they knew best, thinking themselves wise they became fools.

If it wasn't for the Brotherhood, the mighty hand of Cain, this would have been a sorry world. There is a significance to the twelve tribes of Israel and the twin sons of Joseph, Ephraim and Manasseh, Ephraim being the thirteenth tribe who was to qualify to take the place of the fallen twelfth Asa of creation, Abel-Seth.

Demonstrated in Scene XXVI, burial of Abel-Seth by Adam Thor, Cain, and their Gothic Knights.

> There were eleven
> Of the Asas all told
> When Baldr (Abel-Seth) kneed down
> On the baneful tope
> They lifted up Vali
> Worthily, without vengeance
> Their own brother,
> Slowly him, the hand slain!

Cain or St. Michael has finally slain Abel or Satan. As you see there are only eleven Asas all told at the burial. Cain, or St. Michael, the thirteenth Asa has qualified to take the place of the twelfth: Abel, as ruler of this world.

St. Michael is personified as Ephraim, the thirteenth tribe of Israel. Ephraim as a nation is the United States, every nation of the world is included in her, as she is defined as a multitude of nations. This isn't yet but it will be as soon as the light of truth shines into our cellars.

Eleven of the twelve tribes of Israel were to disperse among the nations and disappear as it were. The twelfth Juda was to remain visible wherever he went. This was done intentionally. If the tribe of Juda had been assimilated into the nations of the world and disappeared from view, we would be left in this later time with no clues as to the purpose or plan being worked out here below.

It seems to be a common belief among the nations of the world, and even the American and British, that the tribe of Juda the Jews have been persecuted throughout history because they didn't accept Christ. This does not really make logical sense. If the Jews were to be persecuted for crucifying Christ, they would be persecuted by their brothers, the British, American and some north European countries. But they were not, they were persecuted by the non-Aryan races. Nazi Germany under Hitler, the greatest atrocity of all history, in the name of the Aryan race which is absurd as the Germans are of the Semitic Vandals. The round head of the Alpine or Celtic race, non-Aryan (page 134, *Phoenicians origin of Britons and Scots)* and the Jews are of the tribe of Israel who are Aryan. The truth has been twisted again by the influence of Abel-Seth. If they were persecuted for the crucifixion of Christ what manner of Christianity would have done such an abominable atrocity? There have been many heinous crimes committed in the name of Christianity, no doubt under the guidance of Righteous Abel as stated in Heb 11:4.

If we wish to understand why the Jews are persecuted and by whom we can look into Gen 4:15. But first we should read what S. H. Hooke in *Peakas Bible Commentary* has to say about the Book of Genesis. He claims myths had a function in the story of creation which is no doubt true and also that there are two strands of traditions, the Jahveh and Elohim, which indicate that the history of the people was written from two different points of view. Probably, as stated before, the Aryan and Edenite points of view. And again in the tenth century B.C. compiled and edited by yet another factor, the priesthood. Knowing this we have to separate the strands to regain the truth. We must also remember that these priests recorded the scriptures as they, as men, perceived it. Mark 7:7— ". . . teaching as doctrines the precepts of men."

If we look at the scriptures in the light of what we have seen in the Edda we may get a better understanding. If we look at Gen. 4:15—"Then the Lord said to him (Cain) not so! If anyone slays Cain, vengeance shall be taken on him seven fold. And the Lord put a mark on Cain, lest any whom came upon him should kill him." God does not promise not to let anyone harm Cain or his descendants but he will take vengeance on any that do. Cain is made to say in Gen 4:14—"Behold thou has driven me this day away from the ground and from they face I shall be hidden and I shall be a fugitive and a wanderer on the earth, and whoever finds me shall slay me." But then God blessed him with his mark.

So if we understand what really happened we see that God blessed and commended Cain for slaying Abel or Baldr, or St. Michael slaying Apollyon, and commissioned him to travel throughout the world uplifting and guiding the nations. The people whom Cain was afraid were going to kill him were the Edenite tribes of the wolf and serpent totems. Why? Because Jacob's blessings, Gen 49:9, said Juda would be a powerful people and would have power over the Edenites and would lend strength and have close affiliations with Joseph through the tribes of Ephraiman Manasseh as in Gen 49:11. Binding his foal to the vine (that is the house of Israel) and his ass's colt to the choice vine, which is Joseph, Ephraim, and Manasseh, thus forming a federation of the world. The Edenites resent this and will do all they can to thwart the plan.

Whatever plan for the uplifting and advancement of man is set in motion by Adam Thor and the Brotherhood, Abel-Seth introduces a counterfeit plan. In this case to offset the vine, or the Brotherhood, whose job it is to spread through all the nations with their superior ability which was prophesied for them to gain control of a large portion of the world's wealth which was to be used as a power to influence governments, maintain peace and for the general benefit of mankind. Abel-Seth has brought forth another vine, more commonly referred to as an Octopus with its tentacles spreading out through all nations, especially America, from his ancient seat of power in Italy and Sicily. The Mafia or organized crime controlling vast amounts of money gained from all that is evil. The drug trade, white slavery, pornography, gambling and extortion, maligning the right use of money, making it appear that money is evil, thus another example of Abel's promise to slander and malign the Goths.

It becomes very confusing and hard to determine clean money from dirty money. Especially after it has been laundered and is re-invested in what appears to be legitimate business. Also it is most confusing when the Vatican is suspect in the laundering of over a billion dollars through their bank (which was brought to light by the sudden death of Pope John Paul I). Nevertheless, there are still two powers bringing pressure on governments. We can't put our finger on either of them as individuals and identify them by name, but you can't deny the Mafia. As sure as the Mafia exists, the Brotherhood exists.

Now, the whole point of this is that Cain slew Abel to rid the world of evil. For so doing God commended him and placed a mark on him and all his descendants so he would be known by this mark throughout the world through all generations. God made a promise that he would take vengeance on anyone who harmed one with this mark. Now the battle between Cain and Abel is an ongoing thing, this slaying was for the benefit of man. After Abel was slain he was reincarnated again as Seth and true to Abel's slanderous promises in Scene XVIII he has usurped Cain's genealogy as seen in Gen 4:17 and Gen 5:1–32 and as outlined in Peaks Commentary, page 182, 149 A);

Adam	Adam
—	Seth
—	Enoch
Cain	Kenan
Enoch	Mahalalel
Irad	Jared
Methiyael	Enoch
Methushael	Methuselah
Lamech	Lamech
—	Noah

and made Cain a criminal and a fugitive instead of the champion and benefactor of mankind, and elevated himself to righteous Abel.

We can follow the descendants of Cain by this mark all through history to this present day from Abraham and the Miraculous Conception and birth of Isaac. By this time you have no doubt realized that the mark of Cain must be circumcision of which the tribe of Judah faithfully practices and are known by it throughout the world.

We will look now at an overview of the circumstances leading up to the time of Christ. The seeds of the federation of the world were sown. Eleven of the twelve tribes of Israel were distributed and assimilated into the various nations of the world. Through their superiority they rose to the top and became the aristocracy as we saw with Joseph in Egypt. For (proselytizing) purposes they adopted the traditions of the Semitic moon cult of Eden, as they were always few in number as compared with the masses of their Semitic and Chaldee subjects. Their language was adopted for easier communication.

The Chaldean King, Nebuchadnezzar II was, to the students of the Bible, the destroyer of Jerusalem and as the King who took the captive Jews to Babylonia. To the archaeologists and historians he is known as the great builder and restorer. He reconstructed Babylon and completed the renovations of Marduk's Temple. By renovating Marduk's Temple it appears that the captive Jews were having a regenerating effect on that Empire. It appears that Daniel Shadrach Mē'shack, and A bed'ne go were masters of the brotherhood. It is also evident that the classic Romans and Greeks, as portrayed in their art were of the Aryan race. But with each successive Empire from the Babylonian, Persian, Greco-Mecodonian and Roman, the Aryan element was becoming less evident and each empire was becoming larger and more un-Godly. Climaxing with the Roman Empire embracing wholeheartedly the Oriental Goddess of Fertility with the new birth and remission of sins by the shedding of bulls blood at the sanctuary of the Phrygian goddess on the Vatican Hill at or near the spot where the basilica of St. Peter's now stands. Inscriptions relating to the rites were found when the church was being enlarged in 1608 or 1609. These rites spread from the Vatican to other parts of the Roman Empire such as Gaul and Germany. (page 408, *Golden Bough*).

It had become a Godless world, Abel was once more in control. This equates with Adam Thor being wounded in the head in Scene XV and also in Scene XVII Loki reminds Adam Thor that he once wounded him with his hand wheel, Loki's fiery stonewheel.

You may say that the Jews in Palestine were teaching the scriptures as contained in the Old Testament. At that time there was no New Testament so what more could be expected? Like today, in this Godless world, we have our churches, but we are not being taught the truth as Mark says in 7:7—"In vain do they worship me teaching as doctrines the precepts of men."

If we stop and think about it, if the Pharisees or priests had recorded the scriptures accurately and were teaching them truly, why then would Jesus have called them "An evil and adultrous generation, (Mat 12:39) and why did Jesus tell his disciples in Mat 16:11—"beware of the leaven of the Pharisees and Sadducees" (then they understood that he did not tell them to beware of the leaven of the bread, but of the teachings of the Pharisees and Sadducees) if they were teaching the truth? Apparently they were not. Jesus didn't rewrite the Old Testament so it must still have the same perversions today as it did then. So I feel quite safe to say that this was a Godless world at that time. As I said in Scene XV I will explain how Cain set about removing the spike from Adam's head and nursed him back to health.

If it wasn't for the Brotherhood this would be a sorry world. Luckily for us the Brotherhood was there, they are always there. Moses was a Grand Master and from him sprang a branch of the order called the Essenes. The twelve tribes of Israel represent the twelve Asas's or Lords of Creation. From each of the tribes of Israel there is a chapter of the Brotherhood. They were the only glint of God in the wretched world at that time.

Adam Thor was seriously wounded and it was up to Cain to heal his wounds and restore the world to the true religion of Adam Thor's Solar Cult. So a plan was devised with the help of Adam Thor, masterminding it from above. Of course all invalids have to make a concerted effort themselves to regain good health. The plan was set and everything was in place. Now they were waiting for a sign to start their plan into action. (If I am not mistaken they are waiting for a sign right now!) The plan was to re-enact the life of Adam Thor, his befriending and civilizing mankind, and man's rebellion and his return to Adam Thor.

This was like a play but a very real play. The sign was the birth of the Virgin Mary, a daughter born to a high priest. Cain was to play the part of Adam Thor (making him a king before his time). This was planned many years before. The house of Juda the Jews were to play a very important role. They were chosen to play the part of Abel-Seth, the twelfth Asa of Creation who rebelled and became Satan. In order to understand this it was planned that the house of Juda would separate from the rest of the houses of Israel and the remaining houses of Israel would disappear from view into the nations of the world. But the house of Juda would remain visible throughout history. In order to identify with Abel-Seth (Satan) they adopted Saturday as their holy day after Satan's namesake and apparently they adopted the Semitic language, making them appear to the unsuspecting world to be Semitic Edenites. So that they would not be absorbed into the Edenites and lost, they bore their identifying mark of Cain (circumcision) which would identify them wherever they went throughout history as Jews of the Aryan race.

The Brotherhood was comprised of members of all twelve tribes of Israel, including Juda. By this time all twelve tribes of Israel had rebelled against Adam Thor and were being lured into Abel-Seth's camp. That is what caused Adam Thor's wound. Now we have the same situation as we had recorded in the Edda some 3300 years B.C. Things take a long time to materialize. Sometimes over a long period of time we lose sight of it or don't associate the beginning with the end. Now, if we run back over the events recorded in the Edda briefly, just touching on the high points, we see Adam Thor uplifting, educating and civilizing men of the Lion Tribe of the Edenites. When they were half civilized and half educated they listened to their own reasoning, influenced by Abel-Sutt. In their vanity, thinking themselves wise, they rebelled against Adam's laws, consequently wounding him. Cain, with the help of the other eleven Asas of Creation, set about healing Adam's wounds, but man was in such a deprived state that it took the sinking of a continent and near annihilation of life on Earth to bring man to his senses. Adam promised that he would not let it get to that point again because if he did it would result in complete annihilation of life on this planet. It is of my opinion that if the question of abortion was once again to the vote today it would not win.

So the plan was put in motion nineteen hundred and eighty four years ago by Cain or St. Michael to heal Adam Thor's wounds and restore his kingdom and Solar religion of light and truth. It appears we are in a position today identical to that time immediately before the flood or destruction. Poised, waiting to deal that deathly blow that will put a complete end to this world. Don't be mistaken, Christ's mission on earth nineteen hundred and fifty years ago has everything to do with our predicament today. It is the plan that was put in action nineteen hundred eighty-four years ago, preparing for the time immediately ahead of us today. Getting back to Christ's mission we will see how the plan unfolds step by step.

The point we must remember is that the Brotherhood is the personification of Cain or St. Michael. They are always with us, they are always doing the work of St. Michael. We don't recognize them, and until we do recognize them there is a limit to what they can do for us.

Jesus was born of the Virgin from an immaculate conception. As I mentioned we understand artificial insemination and also embryo transplants. For those who have difficulty in accepting the divine conception they can understand there are alternate ways of becoming pregnant. Jesus was born of the Virgin Mary and educated by the Brotherhood, the Essenes, as we saw in Scene X. He had a very extensive education. Jesus's temptation in the wilderness is the re-enactment of Scene XI, the Combat. After the combat Eve came and ministered to Cain, the angels came and ministered to Jesus.

The miracles Jesus performed were symbolic re-enactments of Adam Thor's achievements and progress in the uplifting of man. The miracle of changing water to wine was symbolic of Adam

Thor civilizing and uplifting mankind. It had the same effect on man as would the drinking of wine, bringing new hope to them and gladening their hearts as in Scene II. When Jesus fed the five thousand on two fishes and five loaves of bread it was symbolic of Adam Thor as the Gardener Goth, teaching the aboriginals how to fish and to farm with the introduction of cereal grains, vegetables and the domesticating of farm animals. This enabled them to feed themselves in abundance, thus accrediting him with feeding the multitudes as in Scene II. When Jesus walked on the water that symbolized Adam Thor's crusade to rescue Eve from Eden. It also symbolizes Jesus starting his crusade to rescue his lover from Eden and restore the Solar Cult of light and truth to Earth as in Scene XXII. When Jesus gave sight to the blind that symbolized Adam Thor's bringing light to Earth so man could see again after living in darkness, being blinded by Abel-Sutt from the truth. When Jesus raised Laserious from the tomb it symbolized an after life, or reincarnation, as is evident not in the Old Testament, but in the belief of the ancient Aryan Pharaoh's of Egypt. Reference is also made to an after life or reincarnation in Scene XII "That will duly speak (for thee) when thou art dead." In Scene XVIII Abel is seen jeering at Cain for heading a crusade with the Ash-cross saying, "They are arms for minors, not for men," as compared with Abel's crusades, and the holy wars of blood and slaughter. We read in Mat 17: "And was transfigured before them: and his face did shine as the sun, and his raiment was white as the light." From this miracle we can conclude that Jesus is identifying with Cain, or St. Michael, as the deified "Son of the Sun God."

While Jesus was teaching the Gospel the Pharasses and the Jewish high priests of the temple were plotting against him, accusing him. The very ones that were entrusted with teaching and keeping the faith, his own as in Adam's case, had turned against him. Identifying with them through the mark of circumcision, making it undeniable that his own had turned against him, demanding he be tried by the God of this world which was represented by the Roman Empire. Jesus was taken and judged before Pilate who was an instrument of Abel-Seth, the God of this world making the mock trial of Jesus of God, judging and condemning God as in Scene XVI.

Jesus and his twelve disciples represent Adam Thor and his twelve Asas on an individual level, whereas the twelve houses of Israel represented the twelve Asas on a national level.

Jesus; the Grand Master of all time, and his disciples representing the twelve houses of Israel; was starting a crusade to bring man back to the truth. "Not for that day," as Jesus said, "my kingdom is not now." This crusade was started, then, so man would have enough understanding by the time he reached the point of his annihilation to understand the truth, so he would recognize it when he saw it and return to the ancient Sun-cult of Adam Thor.

The Essenes, a branch of the Great White Brotherhood or the Rosicrucians as they are known today, engineered this whole mission. Ephraim represents the thirteenth tribe of Israel, the United States of America, a multitude of nations. All nations are represented in the U.S.A. So it is mankind who is the thirteenth tribe of Israel headed by St. Michael the Son of the Son of the Sun God.

Judas Iscariat, a disciple who was picked to play the part of Abel (Satan), must have been a great man willing to carry the shame and giving himself up to be killed for the symbolic slaying of Abel. The thirteenth disciple Mathias then qualified to take the place of the twelfth (Judas symbolizing Abel).

When the Pharasees and Sadducees wanted a sign that Jesus was indeed the Son of God, the only sign Jesus would give that evil generation was the sign of Jonah. The fish symbol in early Christianity was applied to Jesus in his title "Fisher of Men."

In the light of what has been revealed to us in Scene XVII we have an excellent example of the promise of Abel-Sutt—Loki's flame will lick afar, and burn thy backs. That doesn't mean he just slandered them in their hall, but continuously into the future (until he is overcome).

The British Edda, the epic poems and history of the past, has miraculously been preserved in its original, undefiled form; but to get to the point pick up any modern version of the Arthur Legends and see if you can glean the true facts of history from them, even try to identify the good from the bad; it becomes too confusing. So you can see what Abel-Seth has done to the Edda's. What would make you think he wouldn't do the same to the scriptures, especially when we know for a fact that man has sat and presided over the content of the Bible, editing, adding to and taking away, shaping the scriptures to fit their understanding.

The first Council of Nicaea held in 325 A.D., the first of all ecumenical councils, was convened by Constantine (I) Emperor of Rome. The next attempt to settle the confusion was by Theodasius in 389 A.D., when he burned the library at Alexandria so the old historical records could not be consulted to contradict their newly written scriptures.

If we look at the book of Jonah it is only a little book, just barely two sides of a page. How important is it? Why did Jesus refer to Jonah as being his proof of being the Son of God, by being in the tomb for the same length of time as Jonah was in the fish's belly? Is this account actual fact or does it have a symbolic meaning? Did the ship sink after the crew threw Jonah overboard, or did some scribe or high priest, not understanding the message, think the men in the ship should be saved as it wasn't their fault that Jonah was aboard?

We still have the same inference that Jonah was the cause of their trouble, or that Adam Thor was the cause of the flood. That Adam Thor or God himself destroyed the world. We have seen it was man influenced by Abel-Seth that destroyed the world.

Maybe the story could have gone like this. Jonah was the captain of the ship and there was a mutiny aboard ship and the crew threw Jonah, their captain, overboard. Then the south wind blew up a storm. Having no captain, every one was running in all directions, shouting orders. With no leadership, in their confusion the ship sank. Jonah was saved by a fish. Three days later the survivors of the wreck washed up on the shore near Nineveh, found Jonah their captain, repented of their mutiny and he became their captain again.

The actual facts of history don't change. All that changes is the spoken or written account of the facts as perceived by different people over a long period of time. I can't but help associate this event with Scene XVI of the Edda where Adam Thor's ship was sunk, and the legends of Adonis. If the legends of these Gods are pagan Sun-worship and have no place in Christianity, how then is Jesus's life, crucifixion and resurrection from the tomb, an exact re-enactment of the legendary Gods who were in fact Adam Thor. Christians believe Jesus was the second Adam or Adam reincarnated, a vastly different Adam than the Adam of Genesis.

The Pharasees, when Jesus gave them the sign of Jonah, didn't understand the full meaning, they just understood the three days and three nights that Jonah was in the fish's belly was the same length of time Christ would be in the tomb. Furthermore, they still don't understand. When Jesus cast out the demons and they went into the herd of swine that was nearby, he was demonstrating where the demons came from. We know that a pig is the pictograph for Eden, so Christ sent the demons back to Abel and his Edenites from whence they came. (A demonstration of Scene VI, the practice of exorcism.)

Adam didn't die he was only seriously wounded. There is no need for Christ to have died because he was only re-enacting Adam's life. Remember, it was only Satan that said Adam was dead and Peter 2:24—"He himself bore our sins in his body on the tree that we might die to sin and live to righteousness—by his wounds you have been healed." This scripture does not say he died. The Brotherhood, the order of the Essenes, engineered the ministry and the crucifixion of Christ. They know whether he died or not, they have, if I am not mistaken, records which survived the purgings of early Christendom. They knew what was about to happen, they prepared for it. No doubt in the archives of the monasteries of Tibet you will find the manuscripts, laying safe during Abel's rampage, sacking the great libraries and suppressing all knowledge. At that time many if not most of the Jews had already left Palestine and were becoming a wealthy and prosperous people, sojourning in foreign lands as they were prophesied to be wanderers. The remnant left in Palestine were fighting and squabbling among themselves and these are the ones that Jesus referred to as an evil and adulterous generation and they were the ones that Abel had infiltrated with the second strand as referred to earlier.

It has been generally thought that the reason for the persecution of the Jews around the world was because they crucified Jesus. Actually they didn't, it was the Roman's that actually crucified Jesus (Rom or Rome title for Eden of the Mother-Son Cult of the Wolf Tribe and the home of Mother Mary, page 277, *British Edda*).

If any one should persecute the Jews in the name of Christ it should be the Aryan or Gothic race but it wasn't and they never have been persecuted by their brothers. They are persecuted by the Chaldee and Semitic people, but this doesn't make sense either because the Jews would have done them a favor by persecuting their arch enemy, so that's not the reason for the persecution of the Jews. The real reason seems to be contained in Israel's blessing in Gen 48 and 49.

The tribes of Israel had a purpose and a mission to perform in this world. Ephraim and Manasseh, the twin sons of Joseph, were to become the two great nations, United States and Great Britain. The other ten tribes were to be dispersed and assimilated into all the nations of the world with the express purpose of their Aryan breeding, upgrading the civilizations of the Semitic nations. With the exception of Juda, he was to carry the mark of Cain and be a sojourner among the nations and not blend in among them. The Brotherhood was to form a chapter in each tribe throughout the world forming the vine, or you might say, a Federation of the world with Ephraim being the fruitful bow or the head of the Federation. Judah was to control a large portion of the wealth and through economic pressure maintain peace and harmony throughout the Federation in the best interest of all. As per usual, Abel-Seth had managed to thwart the plan. Man had lost sight of his God, the plan, and the Brotherhood. That was at the time the Brotherhood set their plan of Christ's mission into action.

The recovery of the Holy Grail around the turn of the nineteenth century marked the beginning of the final knowledge explosion. We have gained almost all of our knowledge in the last eighty some years. Since that time, with the recovery of the Holy Grail, we are rescuing Eve, we are wooing her back, we have not gotten her completely home, yet. All the while Abel is pursuing Adam, Eve and Cain; hindering them and trying to stop them.

Pursuit of Adam, Eve and Cain by Edenites under Abel

Forwards, ere long, on looking back
One time, Od-o'-the-Inn's son saw
Out rushing with Hymi from the East
Folk-hordes faring forth fell-headed.
The standard (bearer) off his shoulders stood the Ewer,
Waved he the mallet, the murder-yearner afar,
And the ruining whales he dropped.

It seems that Cain was fatigued and weary from Abel's pursuit. Not willing to rise to battle Abel wounded him to the bone.

Wounding of Cain by Abel

Forwards again, ere long lay down
The He-Goat Hlo-the-Rider half dead afore
That shackler (Cain) was scarr'd and
Shear'd to the bone,
And that by the all lewd-wise Loki (Abel).

The routing out and the extermination of the Jews in Europe at the beginning of World War II must have been a mighty blow to Cain's Federation of the world when six million Jews were exterminated. Hitler, influenced by Abel-Seth, knew what was happening. The real reason for their persecution is that the Jews were destined to sojourn in foreign lands, identified by the mark of Cain. So it is the settling of the score of the age old feud of Cain slaying Abel. This seems to fit the prophecy of the one third slain, one third dying of sickness and one third captured. Hitler, by exterminating the Jews and routing them out of Europe put a stop to the Federation of the world. As he said, "If we don't stop the Jews they will rule the world."

This may seem hard to believe but we must realize who has been put in charge of this world to keep the light of truth from being extinguished by Abel-Seth.

Adam Thor on the capture and consecration of the stone bowl, as the Holy Grail, wore it on his head and, if I am not mistaken, as a ceremonial crown worn by kings at their coronation signifying the grave responsibility placed on them to maintain the faith and guard the secrets of the Holy Grail. This knowledge of the past and the secrets of the beginning was not for the common man, it was entrusted only to kings and high priests, the sworn Brotherhood. That was the foundation of the Great White Brotherhood by Adam Thor. It has been kept alive although maligned and perverted in the legends of King Arthur and his sworn brotherhood of the Knights of the Round Table. The reason this knowledge was sworn to secrecy was to keep it out of the hands of Abel-Seth and his Edenites. So the truth will survive unperverted to the end, so that when man is eventually willing to listen to the truth it will be there. Like Eve when she realizes her error of leaving, will return to Adam Thor, her true love. He will be waiting for her with outstretched arms.

It is my belief the Great White Brotherhood today is known as AMORC or the Rosicrucian Order. This responsibility was given to man to qualify him to enter God's kingdom as the thirteenth Asa to replace the twelfth, the fallen Asa, Satan.

This opportunity was given Abraham and through Isaac and Jacob the new Aryan race was born. They were taught by the great Aryan Pharaoh's of Egypt for four hundred years. Moses qualified as Grand Master and led the new Aryan race of Israelites on a crusade to uplift man. The Aryan Pharaohs succeeded their rulership to the Egyptians, thus the decay of the Egyptian civilization and the disappearance of the Aryan element which no doubt symbolized by the parting of the Red Sea as the new crusade and the closing of the sea on the Pharaoh's as the end of that era.

Could the forty years that Moses led the Israelites in the wilderness be symbolic of man's wanderings in a world of darkness until the millennium? The forty years could be symbolic of the four thousand year period between Exodus and the millennium. I conjectured the birth of Laio Tez at 3468 B.C. and substantiated within ninety years as the date of Adam Thor 3378 B.C. If these dates are reasonably accurate and Exodus occurred around 1468 B.C., it would be exactly two thousand years from the beginning of this era, leaving four thousand years to complete the six thousand year week to the beginning of the millennium; the seventh thousand year period.

If the Israelites only traveled one mile a day for forty years they would have traveled fourteen thousand, six hundred miles. That is a terribly long distance and they end up no further than five hundred miles from where they started. If Moses had been wandering for forty years in what is now Isreal, Jordan, Lebanon and Syria, God showing him the promised land just before his death and not allowing him to set foot on it, would be hard to imagine. He would have been wandering through it for the past forty years and if the nation was to grow as was promised to Abraham that area could not possibly contain them.

Any of the Christian churches that claim the Rosicrucian Order is a secret mystical order and want nothing to do with them, or even discredit them, I think, will find they have been preaching from the Rosicrucian writings although not in its pure original form. As we see the first five books of the Bible are accredited to the first Grand Master Moses. King Solomon also contributed to the Bible. He studied in Egypt at El Amarna for four years and returned to Palestine where he built a temple on the lines of the temple at El Amarna and housed a Brotherhood which is believed to be the founding of the Brotherhood of Free Masonry. Elijah, another contributor to the Old Testament, taught the mysteries of the Brotherhood in the temple atop of Mount Carmel. Jesus was the Grand Master of the Essenes, a branch of the Rosicrucians developed for that purpose, and all of his disciples were, no doubt, of the Essene Brotherhood. So it is quite safe to assume that the Bible, both New and Old Testament, was for the most part written by the Brotherhood. It appears by the evidence so far accumulated that all the signs on the road of life point to the AMORC for truth and understanding.

It is the duty of every person to search for the reason of their being. I appeal to AMORC to raise their bushel a little higher and let a little more light shine out even as the light shines from the East to the West.

We are in an age of enlightenment, sophisticated enough to handle the truth. I appeal to each and every one who reads this who has a stake in the future, your children's, and your children's children's future. There is a lot more good news contained in the Edda but that is not for me to say. It is up to each of you to search out the truth for yourself.

I must state at this point that I have absolutely no connection with the Rosicrucian Order. It is only through my research that I have come to the conclusions that such a brotherhood must exist. I suggest to those who are interested in the mysteries of life to write to A.M.O.R.C., Rosicrucian Park, Park Ave. and Nagler Ave., San Jose, California and learn the truth.

The plan for all of this was mapped out many years ago, thousands of years ago. First of all we must realize there is a war being fought on this earth between Adam and his Aryan's and the Matriarch El, Abel, and her Edenites over mankind and the Earth. Of course, we refer to these two powers as God and Satan. When God wins there will be no place for Satan on Earth, he will have no place to go. He is fighting for his very existence. When God has won mankind will be taught by God and will eventually know all and will be a God himself.

If Satan should win he will keep his home on this Earth. He will suppress all knowledge, man will revert to little better than animals. Satan will have no fear of being challenged by man as they won't have the spirit of God to uplift them.

The war will be won by God as he promises in the Edda's, but it is up to us to choose whose side we want to be on and when we have cast our vote we must continue to campaign on an individual level for the one we voted for. With all the Brotherhood has done throughout the ages for humanity, do you really think they don't have the power to hang the rainbow of Gen 9:13 in the sky? The shield of Star Wars WILL become a reality.

The attitude of today can best be explained this way:—The voyage of life is like crossing the ocean on a steamship. Someone on board, a passenger, is offering to pay one dollar a hole to anyone who is willing to drill holes in the bottom of the ship. So far everyone he approaches declines, but eventually he finds someone who will do it. He drills holes like crazy, a hundred holes an hour. Soon others, seeing him, think if he's doing it, making all that money, why shouldn't they? Pretty soon everyone is drilling holes like mad and someone shouts, "The ship is sinking and we are going to drown!" They answer "Yes, we know; but look how much money we're making!"

Let this book be a building block for those in search of truth, knowledge and the ultimate of human potential and a stumbling block for our suppressors.

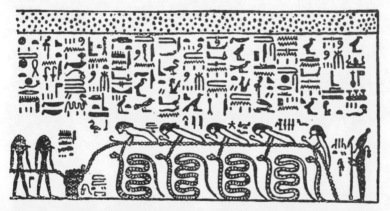

Fig. 35—Cain's mighty hand holding the hooked Serpent. From sarcophagus of Seti I in Soane Museum. (After *British Edda*, L.A. Waddell.)